THE FUTURE OF INFORMATION CONTROL IS IN
DATABASE MANAGEMENT SYSTEMS.
THEY'RE HERE, NOW, FOR YOU AND YOUR COMPUTER.

Q: What is a database management system?

A: A tool that helps you organize and manipulate information or data. You could take all the names, addresses, and phone numbers from a phone book and put them into database software and then extract special kinds of facts —all the names of people who live on a particular street, for example, or the addresses of everybody who has a particular telephone exchange.

Q: Who needs it?

A: Practically everyone. If you are a doctor, lawyer, salesman, manager . . . if you own a hardware store, book store, or any kind of store . . . you need this book.

Q: How do you choose a database? How do you use it? Why—and how—will it simplify life for you, at home or at work? What are all the things it can do?

A: DATABASE PRIMER answers all these questions, and tells you everything you need to know about databases.

DATABASE PRIMER
An Easy-to-Understand Guide to
Database Management Systems

ROSE DEAKIN works for a British software firm and is the author of *Understanding Microcomputers*, available in a Signet edition.

DATABASE PRIMER

An Easy-to-Understand
Introduction to Database
Management Systems

Rose Deakin

A PLUME BOOK

NEW AMERICAN LIBRARY

NEW YORK AND SCARBOROUGH, ONTARIO

Trademark Acknowledgments

CP/M	Digital Research
Microstat	Ecosoft
Datastar	MicroPro
WORDSTAR	MicroPro
WORDCRAFT	P. L. Dowson
DMS	Compsoft
Rescue	Microcomputer Business Systems (UK) Ltd.
dBASE II	Ashton Tate
Condor	Condor Computer Corporation
FMS80	Systems Plus

SIGNET, SIGNET CLASSIC, MENTOR, PLUME, MERIDIAN and
NAL BOOKS are published *in the United States* by New American Library,
1633 Broadway, New York, New York 10019,
in Canada by The New American Library of Canada Limited,
81 Mack Avenue, Scarborough, Ontario M1L 1M8

LIBRARY OF CONGRESS CATALOGING IN PUBLICATION DATA
Deakin, Rose.
  Database primer.
  Includes index.
  1. Data base management. I. Title.
QA76.9.D3D43   1984   001.64   83-22963
ISBN 0-452-25492-2

First Printing, April, 1984

1 2 3 4 5 6 7 8 9

PRINTED IN THE UNITED STATES OF AMERICA

CONTENTS

DATABASE PRIMER

PREFACE

It is now generally recognized that microcomputers have come to stay. Their uses in every walk of life are too numerous and too obvious for there to be any doubt of this. It is nonetheless the case that many people, having recognized this fact and dutifully or enthusiastically purchased this machine that is so essential to progress and success, do not know quite what to do with it.

Working for a firm that sells both computers and software, I am often approached by people who are having difficulties that we associate with the early stages of microcomputing, but who we know, from our records, have had their machines for six months or a year. Upon further inquiry we get the answer, "I have only just started to use it, because I really haven't had time up to now." It is often not simply that they have not had time but also that they do not have any clear idea what to use the microcomputer for.

Apart from word processing, which is still, and probably always will be, the single most common use for a microcomputer, the most general-purpose and most often found use is the database management system (DBMS)—database for short. A database can be made to do almost anything, including, in some cases, rather primitive word processing. Because it can do almost anything, it is difficult to say in a nutshell "what it is for." Its purpose ranges from elementary use as a container for a mailing list or diary to use as a quite efficient number cruncher, or as a powerful tool for advanced research,

1

embracing on the way stock control, accounts, bibliography, and plant maintenance scheduling.

Although a database can do all these things, it does not arrive ready to do them. Work has to be undertaken to set the base up in a suitable form for each application. Moreover, it is not true to say that all databases can do all things, although the correctly chosen one should be able to do what each person requires. Thus there are several problems. One is to understand what a database can be made to do, the next is to choose the appropriate base for what you yourself require, and the third is to make it do it.

This book sets out to explain what can be done with a database on a microcomputer and to give guidelines on what to look for when choosing the base. This is important even for people who are used to databases on larger computers, since there are particular benefits and weaknesses depending on the size of the system. Finally, though not with details or specific products, the book attempts to give some general ideas about setting a system up. A glossary of the more difficult but commonly used terms is included at the end.

INTRODUCTION

My first book,* written after a year spent fighting my way through the jungle of microcomputing, was intended to chart a path for new users traveling the same route: to introduce them to the jargon and the technical concepts; to warn them about the many pitfalls waiting for the unwary; and, finally, to cheer them on with some taste of the excitement and fun to be had during the struggle for mastery.

This book is addressed to these same people and to their contemporaries in the microcomputer world, since they will now have taken the first steps, learned their way around, and be hoping to get some serious use out of their machines. I have been lucky enough to work for a firm of manufacturers that also provides a software service to its customers. In this way I have built up a knowledge of the software available to microcomputer users. The range of products that I have evaluated and used is out of the reach of any ordinary consumer, since the purchase price of such software would run into tens of thousands of dollars. My experience has mostly been with software for machines that use the CP/M † operating system, but the general concepts that are involved when thinking about any software, and especially about databases, apply right across the board. I will usually mention not specific

---

* *Understanding Microcomputers: A Guide to the New Personal Computers for Home and Office* (New York: NAL/Signet, 1983).
† CP/M is a trademark of Digital Research, Inc.

products but rather general principles that, once understood, can be applied to the selection and use of any database software.

The database is one of the pieces of software that is of most general use on a microcomputer, yielding priority only to a word processor, and that only after some argument. It is also one of the pieces of software that is most often badly chosen and then put to approximately 10 per cent of its potential use. One reason is that people fail to work out in advance exactly what is needed. Moreover, if someone does try to work it out, this is usually quite a difficult task, and it is almost impossible to know how to test the software to see whether it will provide the required solutions. Another reason is that the manuals and explanations that come with packages like databases are usually written in a style that is obscure, cryptic, and filled with technical terms used without regard for the level of familiarity that the general public has been able to acquire in the short period since these terms were developed. Jargon tends to be obscure in any field, but the kinds of words used to describe computers and their use are so new that they are not in any but the most specialized dictionaries, and their derivation is usually somewhat convoluted. Thus it is usually not possible to rely on understanding the root of a word in order to work out its meaning. A new word like *television* could be derived from *tele* (far) and *vision* (seeing). Try using this kind of technique on a term like *bootstrap error,* or on sentences like "Macros are useful when complex expressions must be frequently used. They also allow parameter passing within command file nests." That passage is taken from one of the better-written manuals for a database—one of the all-time bestsellers. Moreover, not very much more is offered by way of explanation. I spent over a year finding out how to use "macros" (see below and Glossary) in this base.

I think, therefore, that it will be useful to outline what is meant by a database, what can be expected from one, the ways in which different bases may differ, and which general type is likely to give the best service with which type of data. I have tried to give examples and illustrations of the concepts that I discuss. It is difficult to produce illustrations that are useful but not hackneyed, since constant references to mailing-list or stock-control programs gets tedious. I have tried to use simpler examples toward the beginning of the book and progress to more complex and varied ones toward the end. I have also tended toward a freer use of technical terms, or jargon, as the book progresses, since, however objectionable it may seem at first, you will meet jargon everywhere in the computer world, and it serves a certain purpose—that of encapsulating concepts and ideas—once you become familiar with it.

I should also stress that I try to describe the kinds of tools currently available to people using microcomputers. There is a great deal of work going on in the field of database development, and there promise to be many changes and innovations, mostly aimed at making life radically simpler for the user, in the not too distant future. However, in the meantime we all have to get on with our lives and do the best we can with the tools that come to hand. It is these that I shall be mainly concerned with making familiar and useful to readers.

CHAPTER ONE

Some Basic Definitions

One example of a potentially incomprehensible bit of computer jargon is the term *database*. It is a made-up word, and the two words from which it is formed are not words whose definitions in ordinary contexts are absolutely clear. I had been working with computers for two years before I could consider myself entirely at home with the word and its meaning. This is partly because the meaning is not constant: it varies considerably according to the size of the computer you are used to. The variation is not the result of simple perversity. It exists because the word embraces too wide a concept for all the shades of meaning to be applicable in every situation. Thus, although microcomputer users know what they mean by a database (or rather, what they would generally expect from one), it is not always the same as the meaning taken for granted by mainframe computer users. Nor is it necessarily a more restricted definition: some of the facilities offered by a database on a micro are superior to those of most mainframes, and some are inferior.

Perhaps even here, in comparing different kinds of computers, we may be encountering the problem of definition of terms. *Mainframe* refers to the largest, and usually the most expensive, kind of a computer. The minicomputer was the first kind of smaller computer to be developed, but it seems huge to us now that the microcomputer has been developed. The micro itself has recently had to yield in size to the hand-held portable computer, from which it is coming to be distinguished by the term *desk-top*.

Let's pursue the meaning of *database* a bit further: The word *data* refers to a set of given facts, established pieces of information. It is important to realize that these do not have to be numerical facts. *Data* has for long been used to refer to scientific measurements, but words constitute data just as much as do numbers. A list of names and addresses is data, and so is a doctor's record of his patients' names and addresses and the details of their medical history and treatments. Data can also take the form of scientific measurements, such as figures on rainfall or temperatures over a certain period.

I personally use the word *data* in the singular, as a collective noun. This is the normal use in computing and is allowed by modern dictionaries, but practice is not uniform, and research workers often use it in the plural.

The word *base* is more puzzling. I think that it can best be understood through its association with the word as used to describe number systems. This is a term of considerable importance in computing. Most people think in base ten, or decimal numbers. Computers think in base two, or binary numbers, but base eight (octal) and base sixteen (hexadecimal) are also familiar number systems on the computer scene. In a number base, all information is understood and decoded only in terms of the key number. In this case, the "information" referred to is numbers, and numbers used arithmetically, not just for coding and ascribing some kind of order that may not be based on regular intervals of measurement.

The numbers in the left-hand column of Figure 1.1 all look

number	quantity	base
11	xxxxxxxxxxx	ten
11	xxx	two
11	xxxxxxxxxxxxxxxx	sixteen
11	xxxxxxxxx	eight

Figure 1.1. Number bases

the same, but in fact they signify different quantities according to the base that they are written in. Knowledge of how the base works is the key to understanding the meaning of the symbols.

In a database the "information" can be any type of data—of recordable fact—whether it be a number, a code, a set of names and addresses, or a piece of text. A database can perhaps thus be conceived of as a system whose base, whose key concept, is simply a particular way of handling data. Which database, like which number base, is defined by the original design. You can affect what is put into it and to a certain extent which aspects of it are used, but beyond that you are limited by the concepts of the base that you have chosen. This book is aimed in part at helping you to choose the most appropriate kind of base for a given requirement, and in part at helping you to make the best use of it afterwards.

The next phrase to come to terms with is *data processing*. Like database, the concept can be mystifying, though not as much as the correct interpretation of the term *word processing*. Unprocessed data is like unprocessed food—raw and in its original state, as first identified. Data can be processed just like food and turned into a new piece of information from which the original ingredients can be deduced or traced. A simple form of processing is to enter a collection of bits of information into a file. (A file is not a physical object like a box file but has the same effect of containing information within a given identifiable area, usually demarcated on a disk or tape.) Once in the file, the data can be sorted into some defined order. This is another process. Then it can be indexed, so that we can find the bits we want quickly. These processes affect the arrangement rather than the content of the data; they prepare it for the next lot of procedures, which may alter it beyond recognition. One procedure might take a list of prices and multiply them by 5% to produce the sales tax. Another might do statistical transformations. In both cases the resulting data will be different in appearance and content from the original. Another form of processing might be to create new pieces of data from combinations of raw data. For instance, in a stock control process, the total value of stock held of a certain item might be found by multiplying together the raw, unprocessed figures of cost-per-item and number-in-stock. This is a derived or processed figure. The permutations are endless and the concept a pantechnicon. This explains why modern firms so often need to have data processing departments and data processing managers.

Information processing has the same meaning as *data processing,* but *word processing,* though conceptually linked, is not quite the same in practice. You use it not to make existing words different or to quantify them, but rather to shunt text around. The key to understanding the computer as a word processor is to grasp its power to make accurate comparisons. *String handling,* a popular phrase in computing, refers to strings of letters or characters and the ability to match them and manipulate them. A word processor takes in characters as text, stores them, and can then process them in various non-mathematical ways.

The simplest way is to point out a particular character or collection of characters by taking the cursor—the little blob that identifies the tip of your pen, as it were—to the correct place in the text and giving an instruction, such as to delete. A more sophisticated piece of word processing is to search for a string of characters that matches a string given by the user, and then perhaps to change it for another one that also matches a replacement string given by the user.

For instance, if you have written a sentence (or a whole paper) in which you have misspelled a word, you can pick up every instance of that word by giving the computer a pattern to match—the actual meaning is not its concern—and tell it a new pattern to insert in place of the old one. In this way the sentence "I told him to get out seperate reciepts for all the seperate customers who wanted reciepts" could quickly be corrected. An instruction is given first to search for all occurrences of the word "seperate," and, on finding it, to replace it with "separate." Next, all occurrences of "reciepts" are found and replaced with "receipts." Since computer people seem to be worse spellers than any other group in the population, this is a much-used facility—particularly if it is coupled with a spelling correcter, which stores patterns of correctly spelled words and queries any that do not match its internal list.

This simple matching does not involve any quantifying of the kind usually expected from a database. The very simplest kinds of databases do not quantify either, but merely search in a way rather similar to word processors. These days, however, most people expect more.

Data can be quantified in various ways. Items can be totaled, and frequency counts of a given value can be taken. For instance, if there is a heading called SALARY in a file, the sum of all salaries can be taken in order to total the wage bill, or a count can be taken to see how many people are earning a given amount. Alternatively, a value can be used, against which a relative measure can be taken, and a data item can be deemed greater or smaller than the chosen figure. This is useful, since in a database data is very often selected on the basis of some such criterion. You may wish to obtain the names of all employees who have worked for the firm for over ten years and offer them an extra week's holiday with pay, or all employees over a certain age and offer them early retirement.

Since computers store characters, that is, letters of the alphabet or punctuation marks, as coded numbers, it is easy to use this measure of relative quantity on words as well as numbers. A search through an alphabetical list for all items greater than M would yield the listing of every word, or key field, beginning with a letter in the range N to Z. In this way address lists can be sorted in ascending alphabetical order using the numerical skills of the computer. This facility is not usually available in software that simply processes words, since it is difficult to cram every facility into each type of program.

Actual quantities can also be worked out using a database, if you get the right one: for instance, the number of entries with a particular characteristic, such as the number of patients exhibiting a certain symptom on a given date.

The processing that changes data can also alter the inherent quantities, for instance by multiplying the score on a given subject by 1.5 for people who have a defined characteristic, as a method of weighting the data; or by increasing the price of certain stock items only, or the rates of pay of certain grades of employees.

These are probably the key characteristics of a database, although there are many extras and refinements that make different databases better or worse at their jobs. The job of a database is to provide a system by which data, facts, information, expressed in numbers or words, can be processed and manipulated in a way that enables people to get at information easily, to wring further information from the raw material first entered, and to present it in a way that is attractive both to themselves and to others they may wish to impress. All this is provided without any great exertion on the part of the user. Thus *data* in the context of computing is defined as being any identifiable fact, reduced to a form that can be written down fairly succinctly. The time will come when pages of text can be handled usefully by databases, providing quantitative measurements of text so that the content of, for instance, a personnel report can be scored by a machine, as well as being read and then mentally considered and weighed up by a person as at present. This will probably not be feasible until the facilities of a database and a word processor are combined. *Processing* is defined as the manipulation of data by various procedures to alter either its content or its presentation. A *base* is simply a system in which these procedures are organized in a way deemed by its author to be most useful to a potential user. Thus it is the choice of base that most affects the outcome.

CHAPTER TWO

What Is a Database?

Having defined our terms in Chapter One, let us now examine the concept of a database in more detail. A database is a system, and from that system various things can be expected. The form will vary, and not all bases will offer every facility, but there is a basic conception nonetheless.

Categorizing Related Facts

The first requirement is for a method of categorizing facts that are in some way related to each other. The contents of any file cabinet are usually organized in a way that in someone's view implies a logical connection between adjacent files, and between items within any given file. The connection may be a simple alphabetical one, or it may be in some way related to the content of the papers. Books on a shelf are arranged in a way that is often not purely random, though the logic in a private house will often be different from that in a library. A dictionary will have a different structure from an almanac. A commercial business will usually trace certain links between a stock item, the firm that supplies it, orders for it, and customers who buy it.

When such records are kept on a computer, an equivalent system for relating them to one another has to be devised, and it will sometimes be different from the manual one. Remember that on a computer it is important to establish that there is not merely relationship but also volume and a recurring need. Computers are useful only for situations where there exist the two conditions of quite large quantities of information or very complex information, and the likelihood of a fairly frequent need to use it. If you have a small private telephone book, it will always be quicker to look a number up by flipping the pages than by switching on the computer, calling up the operating system, loading the disk, accessing the correct file, and entering your search criteria. Setting up any operation on a computer takes time, and it is important to establish that the use you are likely to make of it will justify the time.

Storage of Facts in a Suitable Form

Once it has been established that there is a consistent relationship between a set of facts and that there will be benefits from holding them in a computer, the next requirement is to decide on the form of storage most suitable to this particular set of facts. By this is meant the way in which they are organized, rather than on what medium they are recorded. It will generally be assumed that storage is on some kind of disk, though it could also be on tape.

The form most suitable for any given data will be dictated, to a considerable extent, by what uses anyone is going to want to make of the data, and also, partly, by the way in which people have been accustomed to handle the information in the past. Computers can often provide better ways of doing things, but if a manual method is of long standing and has worked well in practice, it is hard, and may be unnecessary, for people to have to adapt to new procedures. Learning to use the computer at all is quite enough to cope with, without any frivolous alteration of other routines.

For this reason, if a database can provide a form for holding the information in a way that feels to the user like a mirror image of the previous way, this should be done. Simple information like names and addresses, personnel details, records of stock, or car registration numbers could be held as simple lists, or card index forms, very similar to their paper originals. The point of the database is then that you can do more with the information, and tease extra facts out of it, more effectively than from paper records, rather than that it is essentially a different process. The same would probably be true of any card-file type of information, like bibliographies or customer records.

When discussing the form in which data is held, it is impossible to avoid such terms as *file, record,* and *field.* For this reason it is necessary to indulge in some more definitions. In any grouping of items of information, the outer identifying boundary is called a *file.* This is the equivalent of your address book, if we are talking about names and addresses, or perhaps your card-file. Several files may be linked in some way, and then the sets of information can also be linked, as for instance in a bibliography where the entries have been split because they will not conveniently fit in one box or file. Files linked in this way make up what is known as a data management system.

A data management system organizes the links and relationships between separately identified files. Within a file, *records,* which constitute containers for the sum of information clustered about one identifier, organize the links and relationships between separately categorized information of a more detailed kind. For instance, for each person in the address list there will be several lines of data or information. These together constitute a single record. The name—or perhaps, to avoid all ambiguity, a number—will identify each record uniquely. The name and various lines of address follow, then a telephone number and perhaps a comment, or some kind of categorization, like "plumber," or "customer," or "supplier." In the original book these will probably have been lumped together as a single item. In a database there will usually be a much more precise organization under such headings as NAME, ADDRESSLINE1, ADDRESSLINE2, POSTCODE, TELEPHONE, and CATEGORY.

Each of these headings is known as a *field,* and one or more fields are always present in a record. Most micro databases insist on the same number of fields in each record. This means that if you have a short address, one of the lines may be left empty. It must be there, however, because any search is usually done on a pattern or matrix system, and unless the records being searched are the same pattern, the information may be wrongly identified. When the names and addresses for a mailing list are printed out, a missing field would cause the category field to be filled with the name of the next record, and thus make nonsense of the labels.

In Figure 2.1, the heading NAME is a field, and so are ADDRESS, AGE, SEX, NUMBER OF CHILDREN, and INCOME. The details under each heading are known as the values of the field. The entry that has been written into a given field for a given record is therefore a uniquely identifiable value. The value for the age field for the third record (S Walters) is 54. All together, the fields on a single line make up a record. All the records added together make up a file.

Num	Name	Address	Age	Sex	No of Child	Income
001	J H Smith	12 Hill St., Boston	34	M	5	10,000
002	P Summers	6 Rainbow Lane, Chicago	26	F	2	20,000
003	S Walters	1 Crabb Ave, San Francisco	54	M	0	16,000

Figure 2.1. Picture of a file with records and fields

Information is usually held and presented in a recognizable form of words or numbers, which are used as quantities rather than as codes. However, there are occasions when a more rigid method is used. A micro database may be used to hold survey research data, or information that has traditionally been computerized already on a larger machine, using the traditional punch cards. For physical reasons—having to do not with the computer but with the paper cards onto which information was punched as a preliminary part of the method of getting information into a computer—the standard layout of a series of linked items, or fields, of information became a line of characters 80 columns long. If the record, or the sum of the individual fields, occupied more than 80 columns, then a second card was added to that record, and so on. To make matters worse, in many programs it was usually easier to hold information coded into numbers. Details about a person's television watching habits would be more likely to be recorded as 1, 2, or 3 rather than "watches 'Sesame Street'," "watches documentaries," "never watches," etc. It is very difficult to learn to think in such a cramped way, but the curious thing is that those who have succeeded in doing so are very reluctant to give it up. As a result there are many applications where data on micros, which because it is entered from the keyboard need not submit to the restrictions of paper cards, is nonetheless stored in lines that are 80 columns, or 80 characters, long. This is an example of the most suitable form for storing data being dictated by long usage rather than any logic connected with the information or the computer.

Collections of data where the number of immediately connected items—that is fields per record—is small, would normally be held in one file. There are circumstances, however, where the number of fields per record could get unmanageably large if we did not try to sort out some better way of storing it, some more suitable form. The most obvious example is the medical records of a patient making frequent visits to a hospital or a general practitioner's office. If the data storage is conceived of as one record per patient, growing endlessly, then there is unlikely to be a database that will be able to handle it, and computerization will be indefinitely shelved.

This is where the concept of data management, rather than a system of simple files, comes in. There are probably several different solutions, but one would be to sort the information into subcategories and file it accordingly. Details of any given patient that change rarely if at all can be held separately from those recorded at each visit. One file could be used to hold names, addresses, dates of birth, previous serious illnesses, and so forth, while in a separate file a sequence of records could be entered to list details noted at each visit. A new record of this second type would be added for each visit. An identifying field, usually referred to as a key, can be used to give a different number to each record in the first file. This number is then repeated as a field in the second file, with the appropriate value entered for each record belonging to a particular patient. It will then be possible to identify all the records in the second file that belong to each individual in the first file. Thus a patient history can be built up using identically shaped records in the attendance file, separately identifiable as to occasion by the information in the date field and as to person by the information in the identifier key field. This kind of system is referred to as relational, since data in one file can be related to data in another, and the connection can be made in both directions.

All the records for Roy Smith in file2 can be pulled out of memory and set out on the screen with the original background information in file1, using the identifier, which is repeated in each file, to link, or relate, data. Thus a history of the case can be established without constantly repeating and restoring data that does not change. Similarly, a medical condition occurring in file2 can be related back to the individual in file1. (These files in Figure 2.2. are oversimplified in order to produce a reasonable layout on the page.)

File1: personal details

Name	dofbirth	sex	birthweight	area	identifier
Ann Jones	4/11/82	F	6.5	AB	AJ0001
Amy James	3/21/82	F	8.2	AA	AJ0002
Roy Smith	6/15/81	M	7.0	AB	RS0001

File2: attendance records

Name	date ...	weight	height	vacc	medicine	identifier
Roy Smith	8/12/81	9.0	20	0	0	RS0001
Roy Smith	10/24/81	11.2	22	1	1	RS0001
Ann Jones	6/12/82	9.5	15	0	0	AJ0001
Amy James	5/15/82	12.4	21	0	0	AJ0002
A James	6/12/82	12.8	23	1	0	AJ0002
Roy Smith	6/12/82	12.4	25	0	1	RS0001
Roy Smith	6/19/82	12.0	25	0	1	RS0001
Roy Smith	6/26/82	12.0	25	0	0	RS0001

Figure 2.2. Relational files, or related files

Another way of handling the same kind of material is known as hierarchical. This refers to data that is split into different levels. These levels may be within one file or in several different ones. A chain of connections can be established, but in one direction only; data at the bottom level cannot be related back to the top level. The levels, known as hierarchies, might be used to separate related data for some types of analysis while holding it ready for amalgamation for others. In practice these theoretical distinctions get a little mixed up, but nonetheless a base is usually inclined more in one direction than the other. An example might be a survey of employment, where data is held in level one on the general characteristics of a whole household, in level two on the general characteristics of the different members, and in level three on the particular employment records of individual adult members of the household.

Figure 2.3. shows an example of a set of hierarchical data

```
Name......| dofbirth | sex | Fam size | SEG | identifier | level
Ann Jones  | 4/11/82 |  F  |    5     |  I  | AJ0001   |   1
Amy James  | 3/21/82 |  F  |    2     |  II | AJ0002   |   1
Roy Smith  | 6/15/81 |  M  |    6     |  IV | RS0001   |   1
x
x
x
Name......| dofbirth | sex | income | travel | identifier | level
Robin Smith | 8/12/61 |  M  | 15000  |  car  | RS0001   |   2
Jane Smith  | 10/24/63|  F  | 20000  |  bus  | RS0001   |   2
Bob Jones   | 6/12/65 |  M  | 25000  |  bike | AJ0001   |   2
x
x
x
x
Name......|  work  | fmsize | duration | pension |  id   | level
Roy Smith  | welder |   40   |    22    |    0    | RS0001 |  3
Robin Smith| fitter |   10   |    5     |    1    | RS0001 |  3
Jane Smith | sales  |   25   |    2     |    1    | RS0001 |  3
x
x
x
```

Figure 2.3. A set of hierarchical data

held in one file, with different types of data at different levels of the file. This makes cross-referencing easier.

Details of the Smith family can be picked out, with Roy

Smith and details of family at level one; details of other family members at level 2; and employment details of all, including Roy, at level three. All have the same identifier and the level of the record is indicated on each one.

The net results to the user of these last two methods could be more or less identical for moderate quantities of data. The moment when an expert decision had to be made might come when vast quantities of data were needed, since the suitability of the form in which a set of data is held is more severely tested in those circumstances.

When data is organized like this, in ways that are slightly more complex than just using a single standard file, there is room for creativity and variety in the construction of the database system. All kinds of technical phrases have been developed to describe the different types of systems. The phrases include such terms as relational versus hierarchical, data oriented and procedure oriented, query languages and expert systems, and others even harder to fathom. For very large enterprises it may be necessary to comprehend exactly what is going on, but in general a good programmer will produce a good program with any method, and vice versa. The essential thing, therefore, is to test the system for whether it can store your material in a way that gives you the right kind of results at an acceptable speed, rather than searching for a particular fashionable style of base.

Reorganization of Facts According to Particular Requirements

The third characteristic of a database is the provision of some method whereby the facts, or data, can be reorganized according to particular requirements. The mechanisms here are fairly straightforward, but there are some databases that do not provide them all. It is very often useful to have data sorted according to some specified criterion, usually alphabetical or numerical order. A sorting routine is easy to write, but a fast sort is another matter, and some database writers have felt that people would do better to buy a separate piece of software to do the sorting, outside the base. This is a reasonable argument, but there is no doubt that a sorting capability within the original base is more convenient to the user. First of all, a separate routine has to be found, tested, and paid for. Secondly, the data has to be gotten out of the base and into the sort routine and back again. This means that the user, whose only concern is to get on with the job, has to learn how to do another set of actions connected with the sorting program.

Assuming for the moment that you are using a base with an integral sorting feature, the power of the sort will still vary from one base to another. First it may be possible to sort in a number of different ways. Records may be reorganized in either ascending order—i.e., A to Z or 0 to 9—or in descending order—i.e., Z to A or 9 to 0. Further refinements can be provided, usually only by a special external sorting routine, and these often relate to the different ways in which computers hold data. Micros tend to hold data in either binary or ASCII code, but larger machines sometimes use EBCDIC. It is therefore useful to be able to sort data that is being transferred from a larger machine in the form that it recognizes.

The next variable is the number of keys on which a program can sort. With micros this will most usually be one. The word *key* refers to that field which dictates the order into which the records are going to be sorted. For instance, a name and address file will usually be sorted into order of surname. There may be some secondary characteristic that is also important to the order. For instance, instead of sorting employees of a large firm into alphabetical order by surname, it might be important to identify department as the first order key, and then sort on surname within department. Thus by making department the prime key and name the second key, you would have a list of departments in alphabetical order, with employees' names arranged alphabetically under each heading. Here two keys have been used. A powerful database will sort under a number of keys, but since sorting is a lengthy and cumbersome business, it tends to put a great strain on the memory and speed of a micro. For this reason a multiple sort is more often achieved by sorting several times over by different key, starting with the least important, so that the original order is disturbed only where it is essential to the new ordering criterion. A database that gives a sort on several keys is a great find, but do not despise those that give one at a time only. If there is no sort at all, then the base must have some other very attractive features to compensate.

Indexing is another way of reorganizing the material in order to be able to get good use from it. Indexing is subtly different from sorting, and is quite different from the simpler search-and-select facility discussed later, and with which it is often confused. The purpose of indexing is to make it possible to search large quantities of data in order to locate one item extremely rapidly. The item must be one on which a specific identifying piece of information can be made available to the computer, in order that the rest of the information can be quickly accessed. That is to say, we are asking the database to find not something a little vague, such as any record that contains a sum of over $20,000 as a cost price, but rather a specific record whose unique identifying key contains a given piece of information, such as a specified name or a part number. In a general search for a characteristic, the base has to scan through every record to see whether the characteristic is present. If an indexed key is given, the base will have an internal logic that will enable it to dive straight into the file and pick out the correct record, usually in less than a second. The various methods, or algorithms, for achieving this depend on clever programming and are subjects of much learned discussion among the experts. It does not matter to the user which method is used, provided it is a good one. Remember that any method will look good with small quantities of data, since it is not being properly tested. Ascertain from your supplier that a particular base has been used or tested in large applications. The best sellers are likely to have been tested in the field by customers, but a new package may need to be examined carefully.

Few bases currently available on micros provide an indexing facility on more than one key, but some do. This means that a rapid recall can be made of all records that have more than one attribute present simultaneously, so long as any given attributes are to be found in those fields that have been used for indexing—for instance, a particular part number for stock, within a particular depot. This would enable a check to be kept on whether stock was available at a particular site, rather than anywhere in the company. The same information could be gotten by the slower methods of search and select, but for vast and complex files the time taken to come up with the answer—the search time—might be unacceptably long.

Sorting and indexing are probably the most important of the methods for reorganizing raw data before any kind of processing takes place. Sometimes there is a need to transform data as well. This means taking a piece of information and creating a further item from it. The method might be to create an extra field by multiplying two together, for instance numbers in stock by price to find total value, or family income by a weighted number for each member of the family to calculate a figure known as income per head. Some bases will calculate and store these pieces of information as permanent fields. Others, more economical of space but perhaps more extravagant of time, will recalculate them any time they are needed, in the form of a report taken from the raw data.

Facilities for Retrieving Information

The fourth basic characteristic of a database is the provision of facilities for getting information out of the original data in a useful form. The first and simplest requirement is to be able to look again at any piece of information that has been stored by the base. Scanning a file, either in the order that things were entered or in a newly sorted order, should always be possible. There would not be very much point, however, in putting a system on computer if that were all that you could do. It should now become possible to list by certain defined characteristics, such as all names and addresses whose zip code indicates an address outside New York City. The number of criteria that can be grouped should be quite large in any reasonable base, although it must be recognized that the greater the number of criteria for selection, the longer it will take the system to weed out the relevant records.

Once a selection of records has been made, it is necessary to be clear about what you wish to do with them. If you wish only to look at them or to print them out as they are, you do not need extra facilities. For many operations, however, it will be necessary to draw the selected items off into a separate file as a preliminary to the next stage. This is because the next stage may involve another piece of software, like a word processor or a statistics package, that will not itself have a direct way in to control the database and organize selection. Some databases do not have this facility, and for most purposes they should be avoided.

Reporting, another term used in connection with databases, has important connotations. In the context of databases the term has come to embrace the notion of printed results, and also results laid out in a way that is attractive to or in some way fits in with a further requirement of the user. This might be the production of figures laid out in a way suitable for incorporation into an annual report or for inclusion in a statement of accounts, or a list of relevant patient data with confidential items excluded, for sending to another department of a hospital.

The user should be able to give instructions to the base about how the reported data is to be laid out. Some bases use the reporting mechanism as the means of providing generated or derived data—the information that is a composite of two or more fields, or fields and a constant. A constant in this context is a number exterior to the data. For instance, doubling the price is achieved by multiplying the price by the constant 2.

There is usually no need to keep this derived information permanently on file, taking up storage space, since it can be produced at any time from existing raw data; thus it is a useful function of reporting to be able to produce it when required.

These, then, are the basic concepts, the cornerstones of a database. It is important that some element of each of them be available in any base that is likely to be useful. In some

specialized cases it may be possible to dispense with one or
another facility, but such cases should be examined carefully
for other qualities that override the deficiency. There are also
specialized systems that emphasize one characteristic more
than another. These develop various names, like Query languages, Expert systems, and so forth, but if you have grasped
the activities likely to be provided in an average system, you
will be able to judge the suitability or otherwise of these special systems to your particular application.

CHAPTER THREE

Some Practical Examples

The best way to get an initial grasp of any subject is to study some practical examples. There follow some descriptions of databases that have been set up to cope with the demands of particular applications, to be used in clearly defined circumstances. I shall start by describing fairly straightforward examples and proceed to more sophisticated systems of data management in the next chapter. These are all applications for which it would be reasonable to use a microcomputer. There are, of course, immensely more complex applications being handled by very large computers. Each year, however, it becomes possible to move whole slices of work previously thought beyond the capability of a micro onto just such a machine. This is probably just as well, since the sophistication of larger computers means that more and more complex areas of application are being dreamed up for them, so that there is no shortage of work for any area of the industry.

Mailing Lists

This is probably the simplest application for which a database is useful. More and more people are embracing the notion of the standard letter—the letter sent out to many individuals with the same wording, apart from the name of the person being addressed and sometimes other small variations in detail. A standard letter is used for something like a direct mail campaign, when a firm writes to all its customers, or to a wider group if it can get the addresses, and gets its name and products known by direct mail rather than by general advertisement. Such a letter might also be sent to the parents of all children at a certain school announcing some event, to all patients of a certain doctor inviting them to come for a checkup, or to all members of a political organization asking for support or payment of membership dues. Whatever the reason, the letter will be one to many, and details of the many need to be stored in a database. A specialized application of this kind may be called a mailing system, but will be a database in essence.

The database will be a container for the names and addresses, and will offer a system for selecting certain groups of people or companies from the complete list. Since any information related to each name can also be stored in the base, other useful facts can be collected into it, and the address list can then serve a wider purpose as well. When limited information is required, for the first line of a letter or to address envelopes, then that is all that need be copied out of the base and used. The rest stays there and can be used for quite different checking purposes, or it may occasionally be useful when there is a need to include in the standard letter items of information particular to the individual recipient of the letter. An example of this would be a letter from a bank to all customers who are overdrawn on their accounts, detailing the amounts of their overdrafts; or a letter to the patients of a certain clinic assigning an appointment time, which would be different in each case.

A letter written in this way could in some instances be done with a database alone, if it is a flexible one, but would more often be created in all but detail with a word processor. Here is an example, with the database items entered in quotation marks:

```
"DBNAME"                                    XX Bank
"DBADDRESSLINE1"                            Main St.
"DBADDRESSLINE2"                            Milwaukee
"DBADDRESSLINE3"                            Wis. 53201
"DBZIPCODE"
```

6 January 1983

Dear "DBADDRESSEE,"
I think that you would like to be informed that your current overdraft
stands at "DBAMOUNTOWING." Perhaps you will let me know what
arrangements you are making to deal with this.

Sincerely yours,

Bank Manager.

For a customer called Mrs. J. Brown, living at 320 Elm Drive,
Milwaukee, Wisconsin, and with an overdraft of $1,500, this
would print out as:

```
Mrs. J. Brown                               XX Bank
320 Elm Drive                               Main St.
Milwaukee                                   Milwaukee
Wis. 53201                                  Wis. 53201
```

6 January 1983

Dear Mrs. Brown:
I think that you would like to be informed that your current overdraft
stands at $1,500. Perhaps you will let me know what arrangements you
are making to deal with this.

Sincerely yours,

Bank Manager.

Similarly, address labels can be printed out. This is done
either by printing onto self-adhesive labels that pass through
the printer on what is known as continuous stationery, and
then have to be peeled off and stuck onto envelopes, or, if
time is really money, by printing straight onto envelopes,
using either an expensive envelope-feeding device or envelopes made in a continuous string that then get torn apart along
the perforations. Only one original dummy label has to be
prepared by the typist, indicating—according to the rules of

the system being used—the exact placing of the lines that make up the name and address. The database on its own, or in combination with the word processor's skills, reads the names and addresses in sequence out of the file and pops them into the positions indicated by the dummy.

Once a system has been set up in this way, it can be used to select by zip code; by alphabetical order; by some factor contained in the filed information, such as size or type of firm, or overdraft as in the example given; indeed by any criterion or group of criteria that people choose and that they have had the foresight to include as data in the database file.

Personnel Records

Another simple use is for personnel records. These can be laid out in much the same way as the mailing list, with a field for each relevant piece of information. In a personnel list for a large firm there may be a need for quite complex information. Promotion to a particular job may depend on experience in a number of different aspects of the company's work, and/or a combination of different training qualifications. The database can be used to cross-reference this data and present for further review the names of and details of those suitable for the job under consideration. If the data is linked to another file, held as a lookup table (a *lookup table* is a list or table of information held separately, to which you go to look up certain unchanging pieces of information), it is possible to score the types of experience and qualification quantitatively, and thus present candidates in some kind of preliminary ordering. All this presupposes a large organization, and the ordinary uses might be much simpler. Records of this kind could be used to hold data about salaries, job descriptions, length of service, vacations due and taken, etc. The mathematical powers of a good database could be brought into play to produce all kinds of interesting figures about staff members. Salaries, age, responsibility, sex, periods of sickness, relative cost of part-time staff, and many other facets of the structure of a company could be cross-referenced using such a file.

Simple Card Indexing of Routine Information

For a small collection of data the best form of indexing is a card index of the traditional kind, stored in a box and flipped through by hand. Even for large quantities of data this can be quicker if you have plenty of staff members with nothing else to do. There is a story about a salesman in India quoting access times on a mainframe computer he was trying to sell, and being shown into a room full of file cabinets arranged in alphabetical order with a person sitting by each one. The access time for a piece of information picked out physically was much faster than anything he could quote, allowing for the time it takes to put the request into the computer as well as the time taken to search for the item. A computer search is nearly always faster, but the time it takes to load the right file, enter the search criteria, and so forth, cannot be reduced below a certain level.

Such staffing levels are not likely to be available in the West, however, and we can assume that a collection of information that cannot be searched very quickly by a single hand would be better handled by a computer. This is particularly so if we wish to obtain not one piece of information identifiable by a precise key or field, but all examples fitting a certain description. A database system will sift through and list all cases that meet the specification. There are some that allow you to draw a layout on the screen, to be used for entering and presenting the data, copying almost precisely whatever layout you have been using on your original cards. Then it is possible to search and select, to index for a quick search, and to design a layout for printing out the information that is different from the one you have used for storing the data. This enables you to pass information from, say, a bibliography straight into a document of extracts, which might need to be laid out according to the particular form of a magazine or article; or from an index of products—say, jewelry or stamps—straight into a catalog or a brochure according to a certain design.

Information might be laid out on the screen in the form shown in Figure 3.1.

Author: Neil Frude	ISBN: 0-453-00450-4
Title: The Intimate Machine: Close Encounters with Computers and Robots	
Date: 1983	Publisher: New American Library
Comments: General, nontechnical, and whimsical introduction to the psychological and emotional responses to computers and robots	

Figure 3.1. A sample layout

As part of a bibliography it would appear in a different layout:

Frude, Neil, The Intimate Machine: Close Encounters with Computers and Robots (New American Library 1983)

This is easily accomplished if the appropriate database has been chosen.

Simple Stock Control Systems

A stock control system is essentially a database tailored to a particular use. As part of an "integrated business system" it has the additional characteristic of being tied in with a sales and purchase ledger, which is the reason many people prefer to buy a customized stock control system. There are, however, many firms whose system does not fit precisely the standard expectations. For them it is usually better to have a database set up to handle stock. People often do not realize how easy this is, because the names of the various programs give no indication that they are similar in concept and execution. Information about stock is simply data of a particular kind. A stock control system is a system for handling information about stock. A database system is a system for handling data or information of any kind, and if it is a reasonably powerful one there will be little difficulty in setting it up to manage, or control, stock. In many instances a specialist would not be needed to set it up, provided the user was prepared to do a certain amount of preliminary work learning how to use the features of the base. It is all a question of how much you want to do yourself, and to what extent you would prefer to pay someone else to do it for you.

In a simple stock control database, the prime needs will be to have a list of part numbers for products that are stocked, accompanied by fields containing information about how many of each item are in stock at the moment; the number, or stock level, at which the user wishes to be reminded to reorder; the names and addresses of suppliers with whom orders will be placed; and other similarly straightforward pieces of information. A database can select and print out a list of stock on hand, a list of stock where the numbers on hand are less than the number that has been entered as the level below which reordering needs to take place, and so forth. The database also provides facilities to enter information—for instance, about new products—and to alter the entries against existing products—for instance, when stock is sold and the numbers on hand have to be updated. Other slightly more complex functions, such as matching orders to stock figures, are not difficult to provide, even at this level. However, a full stock control system—integrating with all buying, selling, and order-processing information, perhaps using more than one warehouse, or items "assembled" from more than one stock part—is more sophisticated and comes under the heading of more advanced uses, to which the next chapter is devoted.

CHAPTER FOUR

More Advanced Uses of Databases

Equipment Maintenance Scheduling

Some databases provide a facility for using dates, but even in those that do not it is possible to provide fairly crude calculation of dates of a kind that makes it possible to set up systems where regular activities or appointments have to be highlighted. It is therefore easy to set up a file containing details of equipment and one or more date fields. The instruction to list all items where the due date for maintenance was equal to or earlier than the day's date would produce a list of equipment due or overdue for maintenance. After servicing had taken place the due date could be altered for all the affected records and set to a date after the next appropriate interval. The resetting could often be a single instruction, of the "replace all" kind, and would not require laborious alteration of each record individually. An illustration of this would be:

Equipment-type	Service due	Done	Current date
Truck	06/01/82	F	06/01/82

An instruction to list out all equipment whose due service date was less than or equal to the current date would cause this item to be scheduled for servicing. When the servicing was complete, the done field would be changed from false (F) to true (T).

The next use of the file, after servicing, would show:

Equipment-type	Service due	Done	Current date
Truck	06/01/82	T	06/02/82

After the file is updated with an instruction to replace the service due date with the old date plus six months, and the "done" flag is changed from true to false, the file contains:

Equipment-type	Service due	Done	Current date
Truck	12/01/82	F	06/02/82

This kind of processing could be used by doctors and nurses for sending out appointments to patients who have chronic illnesses or need to go to a clinic regularly. It could be used either in a database alone or coupled with a word processor for extra facilities, to cope with the repeat prescriptions problem and any other such task whose repetition was connected with intervals of time.

It is not an impossible step to move from collecting and manipulating such information to the kinds of applications that involve some element of real scheduling, and even critical path analysis. This kind of activity is not for the nonspecialist, but a file of data, which is after all an ingredient of a database, is the starting point for these sorts of application. The tools to manipulate data both by selecting on the basis of certain criteria and by processing mathematically are another requirement, and are provided to a greater or lesser extent according to the sophistication of the base you have chosen. In this area, as with stock control, there exist packages that specialize in critical path and project evaluation applications, and very often they will be the best choice. However, there are always situations where a standard package does not quite fit the bill, and in these cases it may be worth trying a good database. You may even wish to do so just for the fun of it.

Research Projects

There are several sub-headings, or perhaps a whole book, under this category. In market research of the "Which news-paper do you read?" variety, a database is a very fit receptacle for the answers collected by such a survey. The questions are usually laid out along the lines of:

1. Which daily papers do you
read?   .... 1 (New York Times)
                                         .... 2 (Wall Street Journal)
                                         .... 3 (Washington Post)

                                                   9 (other)
2. Which weekly papers do you
read?   .... 1 (USA Today)

                                                   n (other)

This kind of survey sometimes expects a single answer only, as to a question like "How old are you?" or "Marital status?" These are the easiest questions to handle, and the answers can simply be stored as values under a field heading. For instance, if the answer to the question about age is 60, then the value 60 is filled in under the heading for age. Or, if ages have been coded into groups, then the code or label for the correct group can be filled in.

Answers to the newspaper question are likely to pose the problem known as "multi-punch." This term, a hangover from the punch-card days, refers to the fact that there is the possi-bility of more than one answer to a question. For instance, many people read more than one daily paper, and so the an-swer might be "The *New York Times* and the *Washington Post.*" Thus the simple entry of the value 1 is not possible, since 1 and 3 must be entered. There are various solutions to this problem. The different answers could each be given a different field heading, but this will in some cases produce a file with more fields per record than are available; this being one of the characteristics that vary from base to base. It might be convenient to set up a field, headed DAILY PAPERS, to be 10 characters wide, and insert the answers in particular slots. Thus the *"New York Times* and *Washington Post"* answer might read:

|1|0|3|0|0|0|0|0|0|0| or, better, |0| |2| | | | | | | |

This is a very good illustration of the reason computer people start counting at zero instead of one. If *New York Times* is coded 1 and you wish to have only 10 spaces in the field, then you cannot have more than 9 responses, because then number 10 occupies 2 places. However, if you start at 0, you can get 10 answer codes into 10 spaces.

One of the problems with any kind of survey research is that data tends to be in large quantities, and it is difficult to get it into the machine fairly fast. The result is that often nonsense entries in the data are created by typing errors or by the displacement of data, so that although the items are correct they are entered under the wrong headings. Correcting all this is known as cleaning up the input data, and many specialized survey research packages do not have very good facilities for doing this. Neither do all databases, but some can be found.

It should not be too difficult to find a database with some facility for checking that the range of an answer, if it is numeric, makes sense. This means, for instance, checking that the age of people in a survey of unemployment is not below or above the working age, or that a study of child health does not include people whose age indicates that they are adults. If such items are found, it may be necessary to check whether the subject is indeed a child whose age has been entered wrongly, or is an adult who has wrongly been included in the survey. In the first instance the data is corrected, and in the second the record is excluded from the study.

Checks of the logical content of answers are more complicated. However, some databases offer the facility to write sequences of instructions, and it is quite simple to use these to check that, given a certain answer to an earlier question, the answer to a later question must fall into a particular category. A survey aimed at measuring the incidence of on-street car parking in a certain area might have an early question: "Do you own a car?" If the answer to this is "No," then it would not be logical later on to find that questions about where the car was customarily parked in the daytime had been answered. Answers under such headings might have been displaced from some other field, or might indicate a confusion on the part of the interviewer, in which case the record would properly be excluded from the survey.

A full survey analysis package will usually have facilities that a database does not ordinarily have. The most important of these are table making routines and some statistical procedures. However, survey analysis packages are traditionally weak on data management, which is by definition where databases have something to contribute. It is possible to get the best of both worlds by judicious manipulation of various pieces of software; the methods for doing this are discussed in the final section of the book. At the early stage of data collection and data entry the characteristics of the database will rank high in the list of priorities. The actual data entry can usually be made much more "friendly," as will be shown in Chapter Five, on procedures for entering data, and the subsequent sorting, indexing, and selecting activities will probably be more sophisticated, as long as you have chosen a good package. Many statistics packages on micros and some survey analysis programs are weak on what is known as "missing values," but this failing can be gotten around quite easily by using a database to sort the records into files including or excluding cases with important information missing from them.

Social Research

This is similar to market research, in that it is an attempt to capture a picture of a situation or a group of people at a given time, but the data is usually more complex. Instead of some simple subject like viewing habits or spending patterns, the researchers may be trying to build up a case for arguing a chain of cause and effect from a set of "indicators." If we wish to prove that poverty is more closely tied to age, geographical region, or government provision of welfare support than to unemployment, or that delinquency is related to family and school rather than to class or district, then the questions asked and analyzed are going to be far from simple. It may be necessary to collect information at what are known as different levels for each record. This means that we are interested in information about a family and its social characteristics as a single entity, or level; in the attitudes, health, and position in the family of individual members of that family; and in the work, education, income, or delinquency facts for each person both in isolation and in the context of the rest of the information.

There are going to be difficulties however you choose to handle this kind of data, since complex tasks remain complex however you choose to tackle them. It will not always be best to use a database, but the work will sometimes be easier with one; if you already have a database for another application, it may be cheaper and more convenient to use a tool that you are familiar with than to spend a lot of money for another that will take time to learn to use effectively. A database that can link information from different files or different file levels would be able to handle the kind of data described above. There are not many such bases available on micros, but they do exist, and there will probably be many more soon at the rate things are developing.

Epidemiological and Longitudinal Studies

Medical surveys are usually based on the study of changes in population over a period of time, perhaps in response to a particular type of treatment, the spread of a certain influencing factor, or an epidemic of a new disease. A longitudinal study similarly takes a set of subjects and tracks their progress or development over a period of time, perhaps many years. It is different from the single-moment-in-time study, which is more common, because the period of time adds another dimension to the data. Thinking in terms of an array or matrix or table, the one-moment set of data is two-dimensional. The longitudinal data has a third dimension, because against every record by every field or variable there will be more than one entry, distinguishable from each other by date only. This is the third dimension, that of time. There are, as usual, various ways of tackling this problem. One would be to use a database with linked files. The original personal record, giving details of age, sex, address, socioeconomic background, etc., could be stored in one file. In a second linked file the information collected at subsequent dates could be stored, with a record for each person at each date. This means that in the first file there is one record per person, and in the second many records per person, all identifiable and capable of being linked with the information in the first file.

Look-Up Tables

A further requirement might be for *look-up tables*—tables of information independent of anything that may be stored in the data files you are currently using, but that you may wish to draw on for purposes of checking. For example, in a survey of rents being paid you might wish to measure each actual rent against an average for that size and standard of property, worked out on a much larger sample. From this you could calculate the distance from the norm of any given case. Physical and health statistics are another obvious area of use, and so are discount levels of sales invoices for large numbers of a given product. The latter example is from a stock control/invoicing use of the database rather than research, but it illustrates the same point. The information is held in a special file that can be called up quickly and checked for details used in the current operation or calculation.

A specialized survey analysis package might provide this facility as well as or better than a good database, but essentially it is the same operation. The point of a database is that you can tailor it specifically to your requirements, and you can also use it to do other, quite different things. It is usually cheaper than a specialized package, since you do the tailoring; also, because a general-purpose package sells in larger quantities, the price can be lower, regardless of the quality.

Statistics

A database is never going to be the ideal tool for statistical analysis of any kind of complexity, but in the absence of a good package, or of funds to buy everything that you need ideally, it can be made to do an amazing amount.

The base must be a good one in the first place, but given that it has the arithmetic operators of add, divide, subtract, and multiply, and the relational operators of equal to, greater than, less than, etc., you should be able to put together the elementary routines that go into descriptive statistics. I would not myself like to do much more, but since all statistics stem from these simple operators, it must be possible, even if slow and cumbersome. Since in many areas of research, particularly social research, the data is not good enough to merit advanced statistics, it may be that using a database only would save us from some of the dangerously flimsy findings produced by using powerful statistical software packages on weak data.

A database that offers a count facility, to tell you how many instances there are of a given condition, such as people aged 65+, can be used to obtain frequencies or simple distributions. If it is capable of looking at several characteristics at once, for instance men aged 65 who live alone and have less than $X a week, you have a crude kind of cross-tabulation. The crudeness lies not in the answers reported, but in the display, which will not be laid out in a beautiful table whose layout helps to point up the conclusions and includes row and column percentages, etc. All these facts can be gleaned from a database, but would then have to be put together into a table by the user or someone employed for this purpose. Thus if statistical output is a large part of the project, a specialized program is needed. But if you occasionally need some simple statistics to give you a feel for the content of your data, you should be able to get them from a reasonable base.

Job Cost Accounting

This is an activity that is often best carried out using a database, since the most efficient way to do it varies considerably from firm to firm, and thus standard software packages may be just slightly out of key. Files can be set up with information about materials and labor charges, and held in the style of a look-up table as described above. Such files can quickly be called up and edited when prices change. Another file can be created to hold details of particular jobs. The particular method of calculating the cost of a job will be held as a standard routine and applied to the recorded details of any job held in the jobs file.

Time Recording

There are a number of specialized time recording packages on the market, and it is an application for which software manufacturers are often asked. However, my experience has been that the way in which the time recording is done in the package rarely fits the requirements of the customer sufficiently closely for a purchase to take place. This is therefore another area of application where it may be sensible to look at a database and work out a way of tailoring it to provide exactly what is needed.

Time is recorded by different professional groups for different purposes and in different ways. Some firms allow several different rates per hour for work done by each individual employee. These rates will reflect both the status of the employee and the type of work being done. A consultancy fee for work done in the office is a different matter from work done on a home or site visit. Other firms have various rates but restrict them to different rates for each type of activity, unrelated to the particular employee. Several professional groups record time only for their own internal records and analyses, and charge fees to customers on a much less specific scale of values. Other firms, such as building contractors, service stations, or maintenance engineers, need to keep records of time spent on projects to combine with prices charged for materials before drawing up a complete invoice. Some projects on a large scale need to include an element of scheduling time available as well as time spent on jobs, and to check this against plans drawn up for budget and time scales.

These sorts of problems may well be handled best by a flexible database. They are often difficult to solve by any method. A standard-application package is hard to find, and a custom-written, tailor-made program will be hard to alter if it turns out later to be wrong in one or two details. A database has the virtue of being more flexible and easier to alter than either of the other alternatives, particularly if you tackle the work yourself and thus know your way around the system. It takes a programmer to write a program. It does not take a programmer to use a database, or to set one up for an application—at least, not if it is a good one with reasonable documentation.

CHAPTER FIVE

Entering Data

The two absolute requirements of any database are an easy method of entering data and an easy method of getting it out again. This chapter deals with the concept of data entry, or the ways in which information can be put into the system in the first place. This can be the most delicate area for new users, the area in which they are most likely to balk at using a computer at all. It is important to realize that an easy way of entering data is not enough on its own, since a database that, though easy to fill, does not offer a useful system for deriving information at a later date is not merely valueless but an actual trap. Ease of entry is a necessary though not sufficient criterion.

Deciding What Is to Go in the File

The first thing to be done is to define a file structure. This is done by careful consideration of the facts that you wish to store in the file or files, and the ways in which you will want to identify them. Take, for instance, the list of names and addresses. It will obviously be important to have a name field. But will this best be used to hold a name such as "Mr. J. Bloggs"? The answer will be determined by what you want to use it for. If you want to use it for a mailing list, you may wish to write a letter to Mr. Bloggs, as well as merely using his name on an address label. In order to avoid writing "Dear Mr. J. Bloggs," it is a good idea to have a field called SALUTATION, containing the mode you wish to use in a letter. This may be "Mr. Bloggs" or even "Joe."

We now have two fields: NAME and SALUTATION. Consider whether you will want to sort in alphabetical order. If you will, all the Mr.'s are going to be bunched under M, which is not very helpful. Some databases have special facilities to switch initials around, so that you can enter Bloggs J. and have it printed as J. Bloggs when you so indicate. Another method would be to take as many letters of the surname as you think necessary to identify the record correctly and use them as an ID field. This would give three headings: NAME, SALUTATION (or DEAR), and ID. Mr. J. Bloggs would then have an entry like this:

```
ID    :  BLOG
Name :   Mr. J. Bloggs
Dear  :  Joe
```

All that is necessary now are some address fields and perhaps some extra fields for other information such as telephone number, type of business or contact, etc.

Drawing Forms to Use for Entering Data

This kind of record is pretty standard and not likely to require any fancy layout. Some types of records, however, are required to list details that previously have always been collected on paper in a way that has become standardized. Taking details of customer orders is an example of a procedure with an established routine. It is quite common to use a paper form that has the headings spread out in a long line, with subsequent entries just below, rather than listing items in a vertical format.

It is simple to design an entry form that will appear on the screen and prompt the user to enter data in a layout like this,

Order No.	Cust No.	Item	Color	Size	Qty	Description	Price/Item	Total
123	33	34	red	M	2	Jersey	5.00	10.00
124	33	23	white	S	5	Dress	20.00	100.00
125	34	12	black	L	10	Tights	2.00	20.00

Figure 5.1. A sample order form

similar to one that has always been used, or that is thought desirable in a new situation in order to make the entry easy. The facility provided to do this is often referred to as a *form generator*. It enables the user to generate a form to appear on the screen as an image of a paper form. The cursor—the little blob that indicates where the next character will be written, that acts as the point of your pen or the next space for the typewriter key to hit—guides the user through the form and jumps to the next field as the entry in one field is completed. The user is led round the screen from heading to heading in the order in which entries are to be made.

Setting Field Attributes

It may be possible to set certain field attributes, removing some of the necessity to ensure accuracy from the user and giving it to the machine. A field might have an attribute given to it that makes an entry obligatory. The item of information is perhaps so important, such as a customer number against an order, that failure to fill it in will make nonsense of the data. By setting to the customer number field an attribute that does not allow the cursor to pass on to the subsequent heading until an entry has been made under this one, an entry of some kind is forced on the user. Similarly, a range between which numbers must fall, or a list on which they must be found, can be set as an attribute. Increasing the order number automatically by one for each additional record is a way of setting an attribute that does not allow the user to enter duplicate order numbers in error.

Another way of affecting the values that can be taken in as data is by instructing the program to accept only values it has first checked for and found on a list of acceptable entries typed in at an earlier stage by the user or designer. For instance, for an entry under the heading SUBSCRIPTION there may be only four possible entries. The actual entry by the operator can be checked against the list and validated for probability, if not guaranteed correctness. If the list is too long to be held locally, it can be held in a file as a sort of look-up table of possibilities, and the entry routine will look in the file for permitted values. The application of these kinds of techniques is widespread, although the examples given are confined to one field of operation.

Default Values

Setting attributes and validating the entries to fields is one type of provision to assist swift and accurate entry of data. Another is the provision of default values. A default value is a value assumed by the system in default of one being supplied by the user. In this way a value is entered into a field automatically by the database system, and only if you wish to change it do you overwrite the original. This facility can be useful to speed up entries where a particular answer is much more likely than any other, and it can also be used in survey work to provide a set "missing value" for answers that are missing for one reason or another. It is very common in survey work to use 9 for this, so that any field for which an answer cannot be found is filled in as 9, or 99, or 999, etc., according to the size of the field. Interviewers often just leave these fields blank, and so it is difficult to manipulate the data correctly, since some software insert a 0 for a blank and some do not. In any case blanks are a bit wild and unpredictable, so it is better to have an actual value. Then you can pick out all records that do not have the missing value, or a value that indicates data is missing, and do your statistics on the good ones only.

Calculating the Size of a Given File in Terms of Disk Storage Space

It is important to remember, when you are calculating how much space a particular file will take on a disk (in order to work out that size of disk you are going to need), that the screen headings and spacings can usually be quite lavish without taking up more than a fractional amount of disk storage space, since they will be held as a single set of headings or a single form, which is cleared and overwritten as each record is entered.

On the other hand, it is necessary to calculate fairly carefully the space that will be taken up by the actual data. Assume for the present that the data will be held in what is called ASCII format. This is not a very economical way of holding numeric data, but it is the form in which it is easiest to transfer information from one piece of software or type of computer to another, and so is probably the commonest way of holding it. In this case each character, be it letter or number, will take up one byte. The word DATABASE will take up 8 bytes. A field for a name that is expected to be up to 30 characters long will take up 30 bytes, usually regardless of whether it is filled with letters or not, since spaces count. The room on a disk—or the space available for your data to be written into—will be given in kilobytes (bytes counted in thousands), and should be made known to you and be part of the selection criteria when buying a machine. The amount of space a file will take up is the number of bytes, or characters, for each record, multiplied by the number of records you expect to hold eventually. A list of names and addresses that has 6 fields of 30 characters and 2 of ten characters takes up 200 bytes. If you hope to have ten thousand names and addresses you will need 2,000,000 bytes, which is 2000K (kilobytes), or 2 megabytes. This will not fit onto most currently available floppy disks and may require a Winchester, or hard disk. On the other hand, one thousand records would fit quite nicely on most well-formatted floppies, and since they are cheaper it is a better option if cost is a relevant consideration.

Disk space

The formatting of disks is not done by the makers of the disks but by the makers of your machine, and there is a great variety. This leaves you with the responsibility of choosing one with a reasonable storage capacity. Some undeservedly popular machines have poor storage capacity, so beware.

Batch Entries

If there is a large amount of data to be entered, it is often desirable to do it by what is called batch entry. This means typing in the data in the fastest possible way, sometimes without pausing to check for errors or consistency. Such data will usually be put into a temporary file and transferred later to the main storage file, after the procedure of checking has been carried out in a more leisurely fashion by routines that, once they are running, operate without human intervention and thus do not waste anyone's time. Since data usually has to be entered manually, it is almost always slow and laborious even at the best of times, and even when carried out by experienced and fast typists or data preparation specialists. Thus it is expensive and boring to have to pause after each item while accuracy is checked, and much better to divide the action into two processes. A batch processing facility is not a feature of all databases and very often will not be necessary, but where it is you should ascertain that the provision fits the need.

Altering the Size and Shape of Records at a Later Date

This is not strictly speaking a part of data entry, but it has such an important effect on the future of any data that I shall mention it here. It is very difficult when first setting up a file to be absolutely certain that you have thought of and provided for every possible need, either now or in the future. Imagine the horrors of designing a file, entering ten thousand records, and then realizing that you have omitted an important field from the record. At one time there was nothing to do but start all over again. Now such nightmares are unnecessary. Any reputable base will allow you to add extra fields to the record—within the allowed maximum, of course—and many will also allow you to expand or contract the width of an actual field. If, for instance, you forget to put a telephone number field in your mailing list file, it will be possible to add one. If, forgetting that it sometimes requires more than ten digits to dial outside an area code, you fail to allow enough space in the telephone field, you can expand this when it become necessary. All of this makes life much less hazardous for the designer of the system, and reduces the risk that masses of data may have to be re-entered if it becomes necessary to alter the system in any way.

Closing Files and Backup

Usually when a session of entering or editing data in a file is finished, the program or the operating system takes care of closing the files properly, and therefore your first appreciation that this is a necessary procedure may not occur until disaster strikes and a file is ruined and data lost irretrievably. It is very important to find out what the procedures are in any package you buy. Some are irritatingly sensitive to files being left open, and data is hard to restore, even from backup, without time-consuming operations that a user should not have to indulge in. The reason is that programming languages vary in their mechanisms for handling files. If data is important, then it is also important to note when a session has not been properly finished, perhaps because of a power failure or some other emergency. On occasions like that, it will probably be necessary to jettison the current session's work and start again where it was left the previous time. It is important that restoration from backup be a simple process, preferably just copying over the last session's completed file.

Security Against Loss of Data

This brings us to the topic of backup and security. I use the term *security* to refer to securing the data from loss, rather than from piracy or illegal access. It is absolutely essential to make backup copies of all data that has been entered during any given session. The best practice is to have at least two extra copies and to copy onto the two backup disks alternately, so that if, unknown to you, your master becomes corrupted, you are not overwriting the last session's data with a corrupt file. The sequence is as follows:

1. Day 1: Disk 1 (master) is brought up to date (data entry).
2. Day 1: Disks 2 and 3 (copies) are copied from disk 1.
3. Day 2: Disk 1 is brought up to date (data entry).
4. Day 2: Disk 2 is used for backup by copying from disk 1.
5. Day 3: Disk 1 is brought up to date (data entry).
6. Day 3: Disk 3 is used for backup by copying from disk 1.
7. Day 4: Disk 1 is brought up to date (data entry).
8. Day 4: Disk 2 is used for backup by copying from disk 1.

Now, if it turns out that during the data entry of day 3 the disk, unknown to you, became corrupted to the point of being unreadable for part of the file, and, unaware of this, you copied it dutifully onto disk 3, when you access the file again on day 4 and discover it to be unreadable, you will still have the work from day 2 on disk 2, since you backed up onto disk 3, not disk 2. This kind of circular system is very important as a safety net against ruining data even when taking proper precautionary procedures. Moreover, even if you are confident of your own skills and efficiency, it is always necessary to anticipate problems beyond your control—for instance, with the power supply. People working in difficult or critical situations can have a power supply backed up by battery to minimize the dangers of this.

The other essential procedure is to make sure that if, as is likely, the data you are entering is being stored temporarily in immediate memory and not permanently on disk, a quick save-to-disk operation can be performed. This temporary saving of data should be carried out every ten minutes or so. This lesson is always learned the hard way if good practice is not set up right from the moment of first using a computer. Routines for quick save-to-disk should exist within the database software, but it is very probable that putting extra backup copies of the data onto disks will be left to you and the operating system to sort out. This is another reason why you need to learn a little more than how to operate a given package, since in this instance the operating system is involved.

Security Against Access by Unauthorized People

Securing confidential files so that the wrong people cannot get at them and alter, destroy, or simply read them is not yet a very well developed art in microcomputing. In any case, files are less vulnerable than on a larger machine. In the case of data held on a mainframe, there are large numbers of people with a right to use the machine. Some of these people probably do not find it difficult to crack the security codes on any given file and read the data. Moreover, because of the telephone link to distant terminals, there is an opportunity for people without even a legal right to use the machine to get into the system and roam around electronically at random. If a microcomputer were not fitted with an auto dialing system, a burglar would have to be able to get at the machine physically, and would also, in the case of floppy disks, have to be able to find the disks and load them up, since nothing is held permanently in the machine. Passwords can be written into the software, and a good base will give the opportunity to do that. A password has never yet deterred a computer expert, to whom the stuff of life is codes, but it will stop the average person from reading or altering files. A great deal of software is being developed to help protect data and programs from theft and tampering. Moreover, the more sophisticated operating systems, particularly those developed to cope with more than one person using a processor, or several processors linked, or "networked," together, have begun to come up with solutions to this problem.

Entering data is one of the most time-consuming and boring aspects of computing. It is difficult to see how a real solution can ever be developed, since even reading data off forms would be slow, though not as slow as typing it in. Databases vary greatly in the facilities they offer to ease this burden, and it is important to investigate this aspect thoroughly. Some specialized packages, including one otherwise excellent survey analysis package, provide such limited facilities that it is necessary to buy a database purely for the data entry procedure. Although this should not be the case, it is sometimes worth spending a moderate amount of money on a package for what seems a limited use, in order to avoid the unseen future costs in time and labor of using the "unfriendly" facilities of a package that may, at another level, have characteristics useful to your work. An example of this might be the very poor data manipulation facilities of the mailing list aspect of one of the most popular word processing packages. Its word processing and direct mail facilities are brilliant. Its facilities for data entry and the selection of data by special characteristics are, by contrast, almost nonexistent.

CHAPTER SIX

Facilities for Retrieving Data

Putting data into a system is an essential prerequisite to being able do anything useful with it, but before tackling the middle ground of manipulating the data within the system, I am going to discuss ways to get data out of the system in a state that is useful to the person using the database. There are two reasons for leaping ahead like this. One reason is that this is a more concise subject area and can, I hope, be dealt with more crisply and clearly than the complex topic of ways in which data can be manipulated within a base. Since I wish to build up a body of knowledge and vocabulary for the reader that will help in understanding some of the more difficult discussions, it seems sensible to take the nursery slopes first and proceed with a common set of terms and concepts when we tackle the mountain.

The second reason for tackling the subject now rather than at the end of the book is that it is the second of the necessary but not sufficient aspects of a database. If you cannot get data in easily, the system is no good, but if you cannot get it out in a useful form, you have wasted your time. This is true of some best-selling packages, and it takes the poor customer a long time to discover the awful truth, since getting the data out is the end of the sequence of events.

What is meant by the terms *output* and *retrieval?* As usual, the meaning in an ordinary context may be understood, but it is not always easy to see how the word is meant to be applied in the context of databases. When you enter data, you usually type it in through the keyboard, as if typing it onto paper. Instead of going onto paper, however, it goes into the database system and is stored in the computer in some way. When you want to get it back again, you have to find some way of sending for it from the computer. The database, or system of handling information, will have some method to enable you to do this. There may be a simple instruction, such as FETCH, typed in via the keyboard. But fetch what, and to where?

The internal manipulation aspects of the base will have the most important influence on what data is fetched, but where it is then sent to, for display, printing, or further storage on some backup media, or for giving to another piece of software like a word processor for further processing of a different kind —all this is provided by the retrieval facilities. These facilities must exist and be able to hand information back to you in a shape that is of more value than the one it was in before you put it into the base to be processed.

The simplest facility for retrieving data is the provision of a listing on the screen or, using a printer, on paper, exactly as it was put into the base. If no more than this is possible, then the base is nothing more than a form of storage more compact than paper files. Unless the effort of putting the data in was minimal and the problem of storing it another way very great, there would be very little point in such an exercise. It is none-theless important to be able to produce a simple list of the data, and not always be tied to listing in the same perhaps rather elaborate way you have chosen to enter the data. For instance, for ease of entry there may be a form that utilizes the whole screen in an extravagant way:

Name: ....   Date:..../..../....
Address: ....
....
....
Category of customer: ....
Comments: ....

To list several thousand of these in this format would take up a lot of paper. It is desirable to "dump" the data in a more economical form:

0001   Mr J Bloggs   74 Hill St.   Temple   Avenue
Broadstairs   Small Business   Friend of MD's
0002   Mrs P Price   etc

1502   Mr B Bonnington etc

It is expected that every database will have some rudimentary method for selecting certain items of data and presenting you with only the ones you have requested. Some of the early databases could search on only a limited number of fields. Thus if you had a record in which there were twenty fields, or pieces of information about each item, it would be possible to select using, say, only five of these fields. Such limitations are now rare, and with most bases you can select using any number of the given fields. For instance, using a base that held information about criminals, a detective might wish to see whether any of the records of anyone already known to the police fitted a precise description given by a witness. All the characteristics could be itemized under the headings already chosen for personal descriptions, and the base could be instructed to search for any record that matched on every given field except name and address, and then display the details if found.

If the data can be sorted into alphabetical order, and the surname of the person being searched for is known, then a quicker way might be to ask for the details of everyone with the same surname to be displayed, and check whether anyone had enough of the described characteristics to be worth investigating further.

Once it has been established that individual pieces of data can be selected out from the mass of information in a way that is likely to be useful, something has been achieved. There are still further requirements, however, and less obvious traps for the unwary. The one that new users are least likely to be aware of is the absolutely critical need to be able to write these selected items of data to a subfile. A subfile is a smaller file containing part only of the data from the original file. Suppose that detectives were looking not merely for a single matching description, but for anyone known to live in a certain area. Or suppose that doctors were looking for everyone who had been in the hospital on a day when it was subsequently discovered that a smallpox carrier had been wandering around. By searching files of medical records it would be possible to find not one but many names and addresses. These people need to be written to, warned of the danger, and asked to come to the hospital for smallpox vaccinations. The easiest way to do this is with a word processor. But a word processor, though brilliant at writing a standard letter with details like name and appointment time different for each person, does not have actual data processing powers. It cannot, therefore, select the names from files for itself. At the current stage of development, it can only address the whole contents of a file. Thus the selected items have to be written into a different file from their original umbrella-like container, in order that they constitute the only contents of the file that is going to be used by the word processor to send the letters. Thus, without the facility to create a subsidiary file and copy selected items into it, there are going to be situations in which the database is frustratingly limited.

The very least, then, that is required in addition to a search-and-select facility, is the ability to write data across into a different file. This makes it possible to use other software with another range of facilities to perform useful tasks with the data. There is also the possibility of what is known as a reporting function within the database itself, and as experience with these tools has developed, this facility has come to be more and more prized. The word *reporting* in this context is generally used to embrace the notion of writing reports, and all that might be involved in such an activity.

When a firm wishes to write an annual report of its activities, it may wish to include in the document some details that have been stored in a database. This might include, for a charitable body, the number of people successfully helped, or the names of firms that have made charitable donations, or even the end-of-year accounts. These need to be arranged in a way that fits visually with the style of the document, and not just dumped as a list of records with fields laid out as in the base itself. Perhaps only certain items from each record will be required. Some of the information might be inappropriate or confidential. Thus the facility to affect the form and content of what is printed on paper is extremely valuable in any database. The same facility should be available for laying out information on the screen in an attractive and varied way, even when it is not needed for actual printed reports.

One example might be a database containing the list of a firm's products. This might well contain various details such as the wholesale price at which each product was bought and the names and addresses of suppliers, as well as information on the product and its retail price. When it is decided to produce a catalog, to send out to old customers and to hand to people making inquiries, the database could be used to lay it out in a simple form (though for something elaborate a word processor might be preferable). However, it would be necessary to have some control over not merely how the items were arranged on the page, but which details of each record were included. No supplier could afford to give potential customers information about where he bought the product at a lower price than the one for which he was offering it to them. Thus these details must be left out, and it is the reporting function that allows you to dictate which fields you wish to be included, and the format in which they should be displayed.

The report facility should be able to draw on some of the other characteristics of the database. For instance, it should be possible to report not merely selected fields of each record, but also selected records only from each file. In the example given above, there might be certain items not suitable for inclusion in a catalog. Perhaps the product line is too various to put into one catalog, and therefore several are planned. It will then be necessary, for each catalog, to select only those items that are appropriate. A computer firm might well have a hardware catalog and a software catalog. Even within those categories, there might be some items that are too trivial, or that change too often, to be worth including. The selection power is needed at once.

If the base has some kind of calculating power, then this too should be available at reporting time. Rather than cutting down the number of fields, it may be desirable to produce extra ones for the report. For instance, you may wish to list items in the catalog and then have a column that gives the price for bulk buyers, with a discount for large numbers purchased. Once you have decided what discount to give, the base can take each price as it gets to that item, re-calculate it in the light of the discount, and produce an extra column of figures. Then, in another kind of report, say a stock valuation, you might want subtotals of the value of certain categories of stock, and a grand total of the entire value of your goods. The base can calculate these and print them out at whatever place in the document you instruct it to do so. The instructions for how to give such instructions will of course be in the manual that comes with the database programs.

Ideally, the writers of the database will have recognized that no one can produce the perfect tool, and will have provided a facility for writing such reports as the base is capable of producing, in a form that will be acceptable as input to a word processor. Then you can either use the report of the data as the kernel of a more elaborate textual report, or tinker with it still further and improve the layout with the extra facilities available.

The list of extra features that might be desirable as part of the reporting process could grow to be as long as that for the ideal features of a database itself. The ones I have described would constitute a very decent offering, and would perhaps add up to a little more than a minimum requirement. Check for their existence and let any decision to do without them be a positive act, rather than an omission, since these kinds of facilities oil the wheels of database management in a way that is hard to appreciate before you have actually used them. Unless there is a very strong compensating factor, do not accept a base that cannot produce subfiles from its main bloc of data or a condensed listing of the contents. Ideally it should also be able to produce listings in formats that are acceptable to other software packages or programs. The precise meaning and implications of this will be discussed in Chapter Eleven.

CHAPTER SEVEN

Indexing, Sorting, and Selecting

Chapter Six concerns the actual presentation of data to the user after it has been processed or manipulated within the base. The three topics of sorting, selecting, and indexing are very closely linked to that of data retrieval, since it is these aspects of the base that dictate what can be presented to the user, and, sometimes equally important, how fast this can be done.

Indexing

Indexing, which has already been mentioned in an earlier chapter, is one of the harder aspects of programming to perfect but a relatively simple concept. Choosing one of a variety of different algorithms, or methods, the programmer creates a system whereby separate records can be identified by some means other than that of searching through the whole file, record by record, until the correct one is found. One of the methods used is called *hash coding*, which is a way of mixing up, or hashing, the characters in the field that has been chosen as the key identifying field in such a way as to make them into an almost unique arithmetic number. These numbers are held in order within the system, and although we can never guess the order, since the numbers are now far removed from the original word that was entered, the order is in fact a regular one, and so any word or identifier can be jumped to instantly, as if we were requesting, for instance, that number 100 be fetched.

There are other methods of indexing, some of which involve extracting key fields and holding them on a separate file. This file is much smaller, since it does not contain all the data, merely the named field or fields by which a record is to be identified, on which it is to be indexed. Details of the particular method chosen need not concern the user, as long as it is effective. The algorithm, or design for laying out this special file, will be complex and highly skillful if it is a good fast index. It will enable the base to locate a record from almost any size of file, up to about 60,000 records on a standard 8-bit machine, in about one second.

The issues connected with indexing are first of all the speed of the chosen method, and secondly the number of fields that the user is able to index on. Other questions might be whether it will allow indexing on part of a field, and whether you have to re-index a file when you add more data items or whether there is a flying (automatic) indexing facility. These points cover all the normal requirements of an index, which does not, and cannot, perform all the functions of a search; that typically takes place in looking for records that match a number of different, unindexed criteria.

Sorting

Sorting is another feature of databases that aids speedy access to related bits of information, and also permits the printing out of lists that are easy to scan with the human eye. Information is probably collected in a way that, whatever the logic of the collection, is unlikely to be in strict alphabetical order. It can be entered into the base in a jumble, just as it arrives, and sorted at a more convenient moment. Data added later can be tacked onto the end of the file and resorted from time to time.

Sorting is a slow and cumbersome business and, unlike index-ing, usually has to be redone after new data is added. It may be important to have a base that can sort reasonably fast, if you know that you are going to need to have large files and sort them continually.

Name	Department	Hardware	Software
Andrews	Hardware	Andrews	Borden
Axton	Hardware	Axton	Donnelley
Baines	Hardware	Baines	Drew
Borden	Software	Daneman	
Daneman	Hardware	Denberg	
Denberg	Hardware		
Donnelley	Software		
Drew	Software		

Name	Department
Andrews	Hardware
Axton	Hardware
Baines	Hardware
Daneman	Hardware
Denberg	Hardware
Borden	Software
Donnelley	Software
Drew	Software

Figure 7.1. Example of a file first sorted by name, then re-sorted by department

It may also be important to have the capability of sorting on more than one field, or key. If so, you will probably have to look around a little, since this is not at all universal on data-bases written for microcomputers. The problem is that sorts take up a lot of memory space and are difficult to do fast. The problem of sorting on more than one key can be avoided by sorting several times in succession, first on one key and then on another. As long as you take the keys in the correct order, with the most specific, or in some cases least important, first, you end up with a file looking as if it has been sorted on several keys. For instance, if you want a personnel file to produce names of employees in alphabetical order under the headings of the departments in which they work, sort first on names. The next sort, on department, will only sort the file into little heaps according to the department field. If the first name it finds with the value "software" under the heading DEPARTMENT is Borden, then that is the first name that will go into the software pile. The next name that has the software tag should be lower in alphabetical order than the first, e.g., Donnelley, since the file has already been sorted. Thus the resorting disturbs the previous sort only in order to put it into departmental piles, in alphabetical order as required.

This compromise is satisfactory only when sorts do not have to be carried out very frequently. It would be far too time-consuming as a daily routine, for instance. This is an area where micro databases are still making improvements, and a good multiple sorting feature will probably soon become a standard provision.

Selection

This subject is at the very core of the concept of databases and will constitute a central part of judging the fitness or otherwise of a particular base for the application you have in mind. The basic notion includes the idea that it must be possible for the base to pick out records according to certain descriptions you present. However, from this simple concept derives a multiplicity of potential uses.

The most straightforward selection feature is to be able to respond to what is referred to as a *mask*. A mask in this context suggests a kind of template or matching pattern that the base must find. Any field that has a value filled in must match exactly, but a field not thus described may contain any value. For instance, a stock control file with descriptions of items in stock might look like Figure 7.2.

Part no.	cost	number	depot wh used	supplier
27194	2.00	30	Bayonne	Mann
27195	25.00	15	Newark	Prince
27196	1.00	100	Paramus	Mann

Figure 7.2. A sample stock control file

News comes in that a particular supplier (Mann and Co.) is going out of business. It is necessary to find another source for parts bought from that supplier, particularly if stock is fairly low anyway. You define low as less than 100. A mask, entered in as words or as a replica of the form shown in Figure 7.2, could be prepared. The purpose would be to identify immediately all stock bought from that supplier for which numbers were low, and about which emergency action needed to be taken. The mask might look like this:

Part no.	cost	number	depot wh used	supplier
		<100		Mann

And it would yield the result:

Part no.	cost	number	depot wh used	supplier
27194	2.00	30	Bayonne	Mann

A search for all parts supplied by Mann and Co., regardless of quantities in stock, would look like this:

Part no.	cost	number	depot wh used	supplier
				Mann

And it would yield this:

Part no.	cost	number	depot wh used	supplier
27194	2.00	30	Bayonne	Mann
27196	1.00	100	Paramus	Mann

Two aspects of selection have in fact been illustrated here. The second example is simply asking for an exact match on one field, in this case supplier. The first mask is asking for a match on more than one field but has also introduced the notion of relative values, since in the number field it asks for all records with a value <100, that is, less than 100. This ability to select using the relative operators—greater than, less than, equal to, not equal to, etc.—is a very useful one. If you have a mailing list and you want to select all mailing addresses that are not in the New York City area, it would be a hopeless task if you had to do it on an EQUAL TO basis—that is, an exact match. But if you can simply tell the base to select all addresses where the town or zip code is NOT EQUAL TO a given value, in this case New York, the task is quite straightforward. The same is true for greater than and smaller than. In the stock control example above, it would not have been possible to select from a large file by exact values, whereas to select by a value greater than the one that the user has decided is the boundary of risk is clearly a valuable function.

Logical Operators

Logical operators provide another useful measure of comparison. A logical operator decides whether something is true or false, is so or not. In its simplest form it can be used as part of the selection procedure, to provide the combinations of descriptions that must match, may match, and must not match. For instance, we might want to find the stock items where the supplier was Mann and the depot was not Bayonne, because the Bayonne depot was also about to close down and would not be needing parts at all. Or where the depot was not Bayonne or Newark since that was about to suffer a similar fate. Here the AND operator, which insists on a given combination being present, and the OR operator, which is happy if either condition is met, are used alongside each other to select stock items supplied by a named supplier AND used by one OR the other of two depots.

Parts of Fields

So far we have explored matching against a whole entry for a given field. There are circumstances where it is important to be able to look at part of a field. This facility is a little harder to provide, though, like many other features, now that its value is accepted it will probably become standard in the near future. In the case of numbers this kind of selection can usually be performed by doing a little arithmetic comparison or manipulation. For instance, you might have part numbers categorized in groups, with the categories breaking at the hundreds mark. Then if you want to sort out all of a particular batch—those that fall into the five-hundred-and-something category—you can tell the system to select every record whose part number is greater than or equal to 500 and smaller than 600. If the operative part of the number is at the end rather than the beginning of the number sequence—say all parts whose last two numbers are 89—you can fiddle around with functions like the MOD function and somehow get the result that you want. It is at times like this that one begins to realize that people who say that you do not need to know math in order to be good at using a computer are not speaking the literal truth, since this kind of manipulation is usually learned only as part of math and is sometimes very useful as a trick for programming or manipulating data. It is usually possible to get someone else to help you work it out, and once you have mastered the trick, it is not difficult.

Matching Strings

If the field that you wish to select on is a character string and not a number, and if the base has what is sometimes referred to as an "in-string" function, then life is much simpler. There are different ways of issuing the instruction, and the precise wording will depend on the base, but what is actually demanded of the base is to find all records where a sequence of characters given by the user is present anywhere in the total field. When looking up a name that is difficult to spell but has a string of letters you can remember—say "ewski"—somewhere in it, the base will search until it finds a word like "Padlewski" and offer you that. If it is not correct, you ask for the next one that can be found to match the string, and this one may be recognizable as the one you are looking for.

Memory Variables

A last feature is the ability to search not on an exact nor a relative nor a partial match, but against a value placed in a special container, a temporary variable. Not all bases have these special storage boxes, generally referred to as memory variables. They are temporary locations, depositories where items can be placed while something else is being arranged and called back into action when the program is ready for them. For instance, you might wish to read the identifying key of a record in one file, pop it into a safe deposit slot, close that file, fetch and open another, and instruct the select or the indexing function to find a record in the new file with a key that matches the one being held in the memory variable. The key is then being matched against the contents of a deposit box, rather than against a number or string specified in the search instruction.

There may be other ways in which you will want to search for and select records from a file, but these are probably the most frequently needed ones. Databases may specialize in speed and efficiency in one respect at the cost of another. Decide what is most important to you, and choose your base with an eye to your own criteria.

CHAPTER EIGHT

Powers of Calculation

The characteristic that divides databases most neatly into two groups—modest and powerful—is the power to carry out mathematical calculations and transformations on data held in the base. The presence of this ability usually doubles the cost of the package, and if you do not require it, it is silly to pay for it. However, it often turns out that you would have liked it, if only you had realized what you might eventually want to do. "If only" is an overworked phrase in computing.

Definition of Terms

Before launching into a discussion of the kinds of operations you can perform mathematically within a database, it is probably best, once again, to make sure we are using terms in a way that is understood by everyone. When I refer to the basic arithmetic operators, I mean the operations, represented by the symbols −, +, × and ÷, of subtraction, addition, multiplication, and division. From these stem most mathematical formulae. When the basic operators have been tied together in such a way as to perform a more complex mathematical activity, like finding the square root of a number or calculating the natural logarithm of a number, the resulting tool or operator, known as a function, usually has a mnemonic label, such as SQRT or LN.

There are other operators that can be useful in the manipulation of numbers and values. One set is known as relative or relational operators. These are the operators that decide not on the exact value but whether a given item is equal to or greater or smaller than some other item or set of items. These operators are:

Term	Symbol
Greater than	>
Greater than or equal to	>=
Smaller than	<
Smaller than or equal to	<=
Equal to	=
Not equal to	<>

There is also often a "substring" operator, but this will not be used mathematically, since it is concerned with non-numeric characters

The third kind are the logical operators, sometimes called Boolean operators. These decide whether a given condition is true or false, i.e., exists or does not exist. The given condition is usually a complex one involving one condition coexisting with another (AND), or either one of two conditions existing (OR), or a given condition being definitely absent (NOT). The basic Boolean operators decide whether statements along these lines are true or false. Fields can also be filled with Boolean or logical-type values. These are useful once you understand how to use them. For instance, it might be desirable to flag records in a file as active or inactive. For this you can have a logical field set to true (active) or false (inactive). Such flags can be helpful in calculations, since, according to various criteria, you can order a flag to be set to true or false. For instance, rather than write out a long string of conditions for the inclusion of records in a calculation, you might work out the conditions first and flag the file accordingly. For instance, the following data is entered with the flags set to "True" for the field OK:

ID	QUAL	CAT	MN	OK
0001	1234	3456	23	T
0002	3456	1234	33	T
0003		3241	44	T

Picking out a record that meets the search criteria that MN is >35 would result in record 0003 being selected. Summing field number 4—entitled MN—for OK = T would produce the result:

Sum of MN = 100

Now, if the flag is set to "False" for all records that have no value entered under QUAL, which is perhaps the Quality Assurance field, and without a positive value there we do not want the data included in the totals, we would get a file like this:

ID	QUAL	CAT	MN	OK
0001	1234	3456	23	T
0002	3456	1234	33	T
0003		3241	44	F

The result would be like this:

Sum of MN = 56

Selecting a record on the search criteria given above would produce the same result as before.

Derived Fields

Databases should also be judged by the range of options they offer for mathematical manipulation. Probably the simplest action is what is known as deriving a field. A derived field is created by the mathematical combination of two or more existing fields, or by the combination of a field and an external number. A stock control file might have a field called TOTAL VALUE. This would be filled with a figure calculated by the base, derived by multiplying the number on hand by the cost per item. A field containing the value for PRICE PER 100 would contain a figure derived by multiplying the cost per item by

100. In this case, 100 is not a value already entered into a field. Such a figure is often referred to as a constant, because it does not vary from record to record, and hence is not a variable.

Formulas

Once the mathematical operators are present for any reason, they can be used in many more complex ways than simply deriving fields as described above. Although a database is often not the most sensible vehicle for carrying out complex mathematical operations, theoretically it should be possible to do so. Quite elaborate formulae are allowed, though they usually have to be written out in a single-line format, as for a calculator, which limits complexity in some ways. You cannot instruct the computer to give you, for instance:

$$\frac{\text{(Sum of values for year } n) - \text{(Sum of values for year } n-1)}{\text{(Sum of depreciation for year } n) - 1/2(\text{Sum of dep for year } n-1)}$$

But you can sum the values for year n into a temporary (memory) variable, call it X; sum the values for year $n-1$ into another, call it Y; sum the depreciation for year n into a third, call it Z; sum the depreciation for year $n-1$ into a fourth, call it A. Now you can write:

$$(X - Y) / (Z - (A/2))$$

It should be possible to nest brackets to a depth laid down by the rules of the base, and some bases will have a few functions included as well as the basic operators. At this stage of development, however, databases are not setting themselves up as the last word in mathematical sophistication, though I suspect that this aspect of bases will continue to improve, since most data that needs math applied to it also needs the skills of a base in manipulating data, and most statistical and mathematical programs are relatively unsophisticated in this area, at least on micros.

Summing Fields

The ability to sum fields across a record, for instance to add a salary figure to a bonus for the same individual, is part of a facility already described, that of deriving fields. However, the ability to sum fields down a file, so that what is produced at the end is, for instance, the sum of all the salary fields in the file (giving the total cost of salaries), is another and more sophisticated characteristic. Summing, which amounts to totaling and can therefore be used on selected categories to give subtotals, can be invaluable. Using the example of the personnel file sorted into order by person within department, it would be easy to sum salaries with a subtotal at each change of department and obtain a view of one kind of cost in different parts of a company.

Counting

A nice corollary to summing is counting. Instead of totaling the contents of a field, this facility can give a count of the number of times a particular value occurs. Search through the file and keep a tally of the number of people who earn more than $10,000, or the number of patients with hearing aids, and so forth. Thus we have a set of frequencies—the first and simplest statistical measure. If the instruction is to find everyone who has a hearing aid AND earns more than $10,000, then we have a cross-tabulation—the second step in descriptive statistics, obtained without leaving the base. As I have mentioned, this does not yet come in an attractively laid out form, but it may be possible to harness the reporting and formatting features of the base to provide even that, in return for some trouble taken.

Memory or Store Variables

The provision of temporary storage locations can be critical to a mathematical manipulation. Sometimes it is essential to do

one item of a calculation first and put the result aside, so that
a second step can be performed and the results of the first two
then combined in some way at the third stage. Also, it is often
the case in a database that information needed for the calculation is held in two different files, but that the base is not
powerful enough to hold open a number of files all together.
The data from the first file can be stored, either as a total or, if
necessary, sequentially, in a temporary storage spot, and
brought out for use with the second file at the right moment.

Mathematical Functions

Databases do not in general provide prewritten mathematical
functions, such as square root, sine, log, etc., but some may do
so, and this would be a further aid to using them as rudimentary mathematical machines. It is almost certainly better to
use routines specially designed for this purpose if you are
planning to do either a lot of calculations or calculations of
any complexity. For simple or short problems, however, it
may be too much trouble to transfer data in and out of different bits of software, and you will be thankful for some aids
within the base. It is probably true to say, moreover, that the
majority of applications, like stock control, simple accounting,
or even market research of a straightforward kind, use very
little more than the basic arithmetic operators, which can be
provided just as easily and efficiently by a base as by some
more lofty piece of specialized software.

CHAPTER NINE
Using More than One File

So far, apart from a few passing references, we have talked mostly about single files. Manipulating or calculating data held in a single file should be a fairly straightforward task that does not involve any very great conceptual leaps. Once there is more than one file, the possibilities increase, but so does the complexity. It becomes necessary to work out precisely what it is you wish to do, and devising ways of achieving it needs rather more of the programmer's mentality than does the single file exercise. However, once you have developed the proper approach, the logic begins to flow naturally. There are only a few methods of approach which it is positively necessary to understand and master, and this done, you begin to see at once the best way to tackle a given problem.

This sounds optimistic, and readers who are generally lacking in confidence about their ability to master the computer may begin to feel faint at this point. My own lack of confidence and general state of panic when faced with a problem on the computer has always been a source of entertainment to my younger and usually more competent colleagues, so I can only urge you to follow my advice and press on. As with other types of learning, it is sometimes the people who have some comprehension of the enormity of the task they are undertaking who get farthest in the end, since, because they are less blithe, they develop a system, and they respect and remember what they have so painfully learned.

It might be helpful to give a detailed example at this point. Take a file in which is data about employment records. The original single-file layout might include information about the individual and family size, and about the current employment status of the individual. A possible record would be:

> Name
> Address
> Sex
> Age
> Family size
> Marital status
> Education
> Professional experience
> Current job
> Current salary
> Total family income
> Name of firm
> Socioeconomic group

A typical requirement would be to match salary with education and professional experience; or socioeconomic group with salary and size of family; or income per head with age and marital status, until some correlations were found or until there were proved to be none. All this is very simple in any database that has reasonable search and select features, even if, as mentioned above, getting elegantly laid out tables is not quite so simple.

Now think of the same kind of data, but for a survey that will demonstrate changes in employment patterns over a period of years, perhaps in order to study the growth of chronic as opposed to sporadic unemployment, and the effects of this on patterns of poverty and welfare payments. You might first think in terms of adding information on to the end of each person's record, so that after follow-up interviews each year, more fields are added to each record.

This would be unsatisfactory for several reasons. First of

all, the records would quickly grow unmanageably long (or wide, since that is how we usually view them). Secondly, since—at least on most micro databases—it is either necessary or desirable for all the records in a file to be the same length, there would inevitably be a number of records with empty fields, taking up space in the file to no purpose. Such fields might be employment details for people for whom there had been no change, or who had retired before the survey was finished, or who had missed some interviews but not so many as to make their records not worth including.

One solution to this problem would be to have two separate files. One would have personal data—address, age, sex, educational level, etc.—for each person included in the study. So now you have one file full of records that resembles the first part of the example given above:

> Name
> Sex
> Age
> Family size
> Marital status
> Education
> Professional experience

The other file is filled with records resembling the second half of the data given in the example above:

> Current job
> Current salary
> Total family income
> Name of firm
> Socioeconomic group

The snag here is that there are no means of identifying which records in the second file belong to which person in the first file. So we add an identifying field—the same to each file. A number is good enough, so long as it is unique. It would be sensible to add a date field to the records in the second file as well, since otherwise there is no way of distinguishing any one of these from another. And perhaps, in case the interviews for the first file were collected over a period of time, we should have a date there, too, since it may be necessary to

quantify by starting date, or period of time elapsed since first
interview. So now we have:

FILE I

Id
Date
Name
Sex
Age
Family size
Marital status
Education
Professional experience

and:

FILE II

Id
Date
Current job
Current salary
Total family income
Name of firm
Socioeconomic group

Typically, some data for the two files might look as follows
(filled in under headings laid out horizontally):

I

ID	DATE	NAME	SEX	AGE	FS	MS	ED	PROFEXP
00001	2/10/81	J Brown	M	45	4	M	HS	16
00002	2/10/81	S Pearce	F	27	3	M	JC	3
00003	2/21/81	P Watts	F	57	6	W	—	15
00004	2/21/81	G Lowe	M	22	1	S	C	1

II

ID	DATE	JOB	SALARY	TFI	FIRM	SEG
00001	2/1/82	Fitter	16500	22000	NT Gas	III
00001	2/15/83	Unempl	0	8000	—	III
00002	2/1/82	Typist	9500	19000	Temp(AM)	III
00002	1/12/83	Admin Sec	14000	28000	Finewear	II
00003	2/10/82	Cleaner	8000	8000	Cityclean	V
00003	2/12/83	Unempl	0	5000	—	V
00004	2/12/83	Journalist	21000	21000	Times	II

There are a number of useful things that can be done with data like this, though also some limitations, as will be explained later. We may want to look at employment histories for the different groups of qualifications. It would be possible to take each record in the first file and go through the second file to find the current employment record for each, thus checking the job at the start of the survey. The records would display, according to instructions, the name, qualifications, and first job thus:

J Brown	high school	Unemployed
S Pearce	junior college	Admin Secretary
P Watts	nil	Unemployed
G Lowe	college	Journalist

In files holding quite different kinds of data there might be information such as the names of health club members and the last use made of facilities, or the names of products and current suppliers. Similarly, two such files could be used to hold the history of a patient's medical treatments, a professional's fees, a customer's account, or the maintenance and reliability of a piece of equipment. This is done by looking not at just one particular but at all—at records in the second file that relate to any given identified record in the first file. Thus the history of J. Brown displays as:

ID	DATE	NAME	SEX	AGE	FS	MS	ED	PROFEXP
00001	2/10/81	J Brown	M	45	4	M	HS	16

ID	DATE	JOB	SALARY	TFI	FIRM	SEG
00001	2/1/82	Fitter	16500	22000	NT Gas	III
00001	2/15/83	Unempl	0	8000	—	III

It is possible to do a number of clever operations with data using two or more files, and the limits will depend largely on the facilities offered by any base. Some operations are particularly difficult, although the reasons for this may not be immediately apparent.

Cross-Tabulations

If, for instance, cross-tabulations are required for the same kinds of variables as in the employment data, this will not be a simple task, as it was when all the information was in a single file. It is, unfortunately, more than likely that, where the variables to be cross-tabulated are located in separate files, we will now find that simple cross-referencing of this kind is impossible, even with databases that offer access to more than one file at a time. The base may be able to do all kinds of clever things like looking at both files and listing data from each against a single identifying key, but it will usually be looking into them consecutively, grabbing a small section of data, saving it, and printing it out with another small bit of data from the other file. With cross-tabulations it needs to look simultaneously at the data in each file and see what conditions exist in parallel. For instance, for the same identification number (and thus the same subject or case) education may need to be charted against current employment status—employed or not—to see whether there are indications that people with less education are the first to lose their jobs in a recession. Or sex could be charted against the same variable, to see whether women suffer first, and if so, whether married women lose their jobs before the single, divorced, and widowed.

If we ask the base to do this, it first has to set up an accumulation box; then it has to go into the first file, pick up the first ID number, hang onto it; pick up the education figure, hang onto it; go into the second file, find the most recently dated record for the same ID number, pick up the employment status, check it against the education figure; then, if the combination matches the search criteria, increase the count in the box that has been set up to accumulate the total of cases that match the criteria; go back to the first file and repeat the process for the next record number; and so on until it has checked through the file. This is asking a bit much of most databases on micros.

Joining Files and Writing from Two Files to a Third

All is not lost, however. It is very probable that the base will have some mechanisms for writing sections of data to other files, and there are several possible ways of proceeding. The easiest would be through a facility to create a third file into which bits of each of the first two could be written, thus creating a single file from which cross-tabulations can be drawn. Perhaps we want to find out whether people with good educational qualifications were more successful at avoiding unemployment in 1983 than those with poor qualifications or none. Then, if possible, pick up all cases from FILE I, taking the ID, education, and professional experience only, and put them into a third file. Now we go to the second file, pick up the ID and job description for the 1983 interviews only from FILE II, and put them into the third file also, matched by ID with the records that have already been put there from the first file. This joins the data to make single records, each containing:

ID:
Education:
Professional experience:
Job description:

Cross-tabulating is once again a straightforward task. In another example, we may wish to see what happens to those who graduate from high school and get a job, as compared with those who go to college, perhaps in order to test the theory that the four-year head start is maintained throughout working life by those who get jobs early. For this we would want to look at the whole job history of each individual. This could be done by cross-referencing age and salary as well as job description against education, in order to see which kind of educational pattern seems to produce more income for each individual at any given period of life and/or date in time.

Outline of a More Complex Example

To give some flavor of what can be achieved with a good database on a good 8-bit (i.e., modest) microcomputer, it is worthwhile to give an outline of an application in use. This is a system set up, and still being tested and improved, for doctors working on a project involving both medical care and research in the form of continuous monitoring and assessment of results. A retrospective analysis will also be carried out when the project is finished.

There are two main data files. One is for taking down basic details about the patient at the first visit. These remain unchanged, unless any detail is found to be inaccurate. The kind of information included might be name, address, sex, date of birth, date first seen, chronic illnesses, and family medical history. The second main file is for records of patient visits. This records things that change, like date of visit, weight and height, and new illnesses. It also has slots for variables that are calculated afresh each time, such as rate of change in weight since the last visit.

In addition to these two files, which save basic data and a history of data collected at each visit, a third set of files is created. It is interesting to be able to look at a collection of visit data for each point in time, for instance on the date of each clinic visit. To make this possible, the set of records collected at each visit is also saved under another name, that of the day's date. Thus, point-of-time records can be looked at for a collective group of patients, and individual and group histories can be looked at from the history file.

Further files exist in the form of look-up tables. One of the variables that is calculated at each visit, and that can be used both for retrospective research and for immediate diagnostic purposes, is each child's weight-for-height. This is calculated by taking the height and weight and making comparisons with a table of values made up from the average values of a normal group in the population. Thus for any given height an expected, or average, weight can be read from the table. The

actual recorded weight today can be compared with the expected weight for a child of this height, and a percentage that
shows the deviation from the norm can be calculated. This is
achieved by having the base hold files of data arranged in
tables, and, as each entry of a current patient is made, checking actual figures against the table; working out the percentage and presenting it onscreen to the doctor; and then
recording it in the various files where it will be required for
research analysis at a later date.

Using a database for some kinds of calculations will probably seem unsuitably messy and clumsy to some people, but it
may not be possible to collect data in a better form, or at least
not one that provides for all the other requirements. Collecting data is so terribly arduous that it is important to wring as
much information as possible out of it. This is especially true
in cases where the data is not merely part of a statistical exercise, but part of a medical treatment plan or part of a business
firm's records. In such cases there is a need for all kinds of
material that will not be acceptable to statistics packages, like
names and addresses, and long strings of information that are
in words, not figures.

Handling data from several files is probably one of the more
difficult parts of database management. Provision for this is,
however, one of the more significant and important aspects of
a database, and for any kind of complex application it will
almost certainly be a requirement. Look into the facilities offered and make sure that what you need is available. It will
probably be a case of taking someone else's word for it, since
a short demonstration (which is more than is usually offered
before a software package is purchased) may not be enough
for you to establish the workings of the base in detail.

CHAPTER TEN

Menus and Command Files

"Menu-driven" is a phrase that crops up everywhere in micro-computing. It is another example of a meaning taken from the ordinary use of a word and used in a slightly different context. The orthodox definition of "menu" is a detailed list of dishes served. From this definition it is a short step to the meaning of the term in the context of computers: a list from which you choose. A menu in a computer program is a list of options from which you choose the next action to be performed by the program and the computer. You activate this choice by pressing the key associated with that item on the list. Once you have seen a menu on the screen, it becomes more comprehensible.

```
                 MENU OF OPTIONS
          1. Create a new file.
          2. Enter new data.
          3. Review existing records.
          4. Prepare report.
          5. Select records for mailing list.
          Press appropriate number to proceed.
```

There can be hierarchies of menus, stepping down through several different levels. For instance, if you choose item 2 on the above list, you might get a second menu, like this:

1. Add new record.
2. Alter existing record.
3. Delete record.

If you chose item 2 here you might, in some circumstances, get a further set of questions, such as:

1. Overwrite existing data.
2. Store in temporary file.
3. Update more than one file.

This provides three sets of menu options to choose from before any direct action occurs, giving an inexperienced user careful guidance through the program and the possibilities in a way that makes it possible in many instances to use a program without having to learn very much or to spend ages studying incomprehensible manuals.

User Friendliness

In recent years much time and thought has been given to making the operation of computers "user friendly." The need to provide programs that ordinary people can use without the mediation of a computer professional has become particularly urgent since the advent of micros, and it is in microcomputing that the lead has been set. The use of menus is part of the effort to make it appear that all you have to do is turn the key to switch the machine on, and after that it is a simple, guided push-button operation. Such claims are misleading. In fact, if as great an effort as that which has gone into programming for ease of use had gone into producing simple and comprehensible written instructions, as much if not more might have been achieved. It is well known that people do not read manuals properly, but it is also quite obvious why they do not. No one has time to read such volumes of badly arranged and incomprehensibly written instructions, so they launch into using the machine badly prepared, make a mess of it, and throw up their hands in despair.

Snags in Menu-Driven Software

Menu-driven software is one answer to these problems, but it has drawbacks as well as advantages. The drawbacks are especially apparent when using databases, which are general-purpose tools rather than programs tailored for special applications. For one thing, the provision of menus slows down the speed of operation. At first this is not important, but it will often become more and more so as the base is more frequently and more confidently used. The speed of operation is inevitably affected by the fact that the base has to keep on fetching messages and displaying them on the screen, and the user has to type in the option. The option gets registered and the base proceeds to carry out the command. This is analogous to situations in which it is easier and quicker to do something yourself than to send for a subordinate, explain what you want, wait while it is done for you, and only then receive a report or the end product. In general, of course, this kind of delegation of work frees you to do something else while waiting; the computer, however, operates too fast for that, but slowly enough to keep you hanging around. For this reason menus, or their overuse, delight the beginner but tend to irritate the experienced user.

Another drawback to the use of menus is that it tends to limit the flexibility and range of a database. Here again, for a limited tailor-made program this is not important, but for a database it is. The point of using a database will be lost in many cases if all that is available is a prescribed course of action. You may wish to handle data in a novel way. If the options available to the user are listed in a series of menus, then there can be only as many options as the designer of the software was able to dream up, or as can be squeezed into the available space. If the options are simply as many as you can create out of combinations of primary commands, then the progression is geometric rather than arithmetic, and the initial storage space will be needed for the primary commands only. Thus it may be possible to develop whole new characteristics and aspects of the base.

In an earlier chapter the pros and cons of simple versus complex databases were considered. The point at issue here is rather similar. For a simple application there is a case for finding a simple database with limited facilities, and a menu-driven one will probably be best. For a database that is to be used as part of a fairly complex system, holding several different data files and being used for a number of different jobs, it would be better to find a more sophisticated base, and it will probably be better if the original software is not menu-driven. This may seem illogical: surely the more complicated the system to be set up is, the more important it is to have the system easy to operate, and what is more conducive to ease of operation than menus?

Command Files

Fortunately, there is a compromise situation. The best kinds of database programs have a facility for stringing together sequences of primary commands and storing them in a file, which can be called up and executed on a single command. It is quite easy to set up such files to hold strings of commands that constitute a menu to appear on the screen for inexperienced users. This has two benefits. One is for the unskilled user, and the other is for the storing of sets of instructions that have been worked on and refined to the point where they are known to be able to carry out some often used activity in a satisfactory way. There is then no point in typing in the instructions each time, so you store them in a file and just call that up when needed.

Whether you are programming by using a computer language or a database that can store commands, the creation of menus is relatively simple, once you have grasped what a menu does. It offers you a list of choices and has, concealed behind the scenes, a set of instructions telling the program what to do next in the event of each separate option being chosen. For instance, if the option selected indicates that the user wishes to add data to a file, and the file name has already been specified, the instruction to the program will be to go to the file, open it, make it ready for receiving some extra entries, and assist the user by putting the headings on the screen for the data items that are now expected. An indication of how to end the process would also be helpful. What the user would see on the screen might be:

MENU
1. Add new data.
2. Draw graph.

On selecting the first item and pressing the key marked 1 the following would appear, after a short pause:

Add data
Name:
Address:
Tel no:
etc:

This is no different from what would appear if the database had the menus prewritten by someone else. The point is that it is easy to do, and if you write your own menus you can put what you like into them. You might, for instance, wish to leave the database temporarily and take some of the data out of it and into a statistics package. First you might wish to select certain records and also certain fields only of the selected records. In that case you could set up a menu that read:

1. Select records for statistics.
2. Select fields for statistics.
3. Exit to statistics program.
4. Exit menu.

Selecting 1 would cause you to be instructed:

Enter selection criteria.

The program would read through the file, pick out all the records that matched your criteria, and write them to a subfile. Then it would "loop" back, following an instruction to redisplay the menu, and the menu would appear again. Selecting 2 would cause you to be asked:

Which fields?

This time the program would go to the subfile, pick out the correct fields of each record, and put them into a subfile. In fact, these two processes would probably be performed in one sweep, but it is easier to consider them broken down into stages like this. The same menu would appear yet again, and now, to start working with the statistics, the choice is 3. The database closes itself down temporarily and enters the statistics program, which is an entirely different piece of software, not known to the original writers of the base and therefore not likely to have been included in a set of menu options.

We have shown that you can get menus from a program that is not described by the supplier as menu driven. Now let's look at the special attractions of bases with facilities for command files.

Interactive and Batch Mode

A command file is one that stores neither data nor a complete program, but a set of instructions that a program can pull over from the disk and execute sequentially from start to finish. The last command can restore the normal interactive functioning of the original program. The word *interactive* refers to the fact that the user interacts with the computer, issuing a single instruction, having it executed, issuing another, and so on. Work on microcomputers is usually interactive, or "in interactive mode." On larger computers, although it can be interactive through the use of a terminal to provide a screen and so forth, it has historically more often been "in batch mode," meaning that sequences of instructions are worked out in advance and given to the computer in a batch for execution.

The beauty of a command file is that it combines these two methods. Some instructions are given in a batch, but within

these sequences of predetermined instructions may be one
that halts the sequence and returns temporarily to interactive
mode, asking the user for some input via a menu or a prompt-
ing question. This prompt may be for some data to enter, some
criteria to search on, the name of a file to write to or get data
from, and so on. An example might be the following set of
instructions:

        Open file containing names and addresses for mailing list
        Load search criteria
        In order to do this, ask user:
    x   "Criteria for selecting names?"
    x   Take answer (eg "zip code = 10019") and
        Put in as value (10019) to be searched for in variable (ZCODE)
        For each correct value found, copy record to file SUBMAIL
        When complete, put message on screen:
    x   "Ready for letter/label preparation"
        Return to menu or back to base

The lines marked with an x involve interaction with the user.
The rest have enough information to allow the program to
proceed without intervention from outside. The wording of
the commands will depend on the syntax—or instruction set
—provided for in the particular database in use.

Using Macros

There is yet another clever feature of the facility for writing
programs with a database, and it makes use of what is often
referred to as the *macro*. This is another example of a baffling
use of words in the world of computing: *Macro* should mean
"large," but it is used here to mean an anonymous term that
will later on be given a precise value or meaning, rather like
a field or a variable. In fact, it is almost the field name for a
field. It can also be a string of commands, or a single complex
command, referenced by one word, usually preceded by a
symbol. The extended meaning must be found by the system
either in the memory or in some other known location. Once
you have grasped what it is for, the macro becomes a marvel-
ously useful concept. You can write an instruction to the

database telling it to load a file referred to at this stage not by name but by macro-identifier. An earlier instruction might have asked the user which file he wished to use for the current operation. The answer would then be slotted into the container provided by the macro and could therefore vary with each run of the program. Thus you could use the same command file to run a direct mailing from a series of different data files, simply varying the file name each time. An example might be:

```
Ask user "Name of file from which to select records?"
Ask user "On what criteria do you wish to select names etc for direct
mailing?"
Ask user "Name of new file to write these names to?"
Call up <macro-file> to use for direct mailing
Select records on <macro criteria>
Write selected records to <macro new file>
Prepare labels using <macro new file>
```

Using the answers provided by a user, we might have:

```
Ask user "Name of file from which to select records?"
INPUT = "CUSTOMER"
Ask user "On what criteria do you wish to select names etc for direct
mailing?"
INPUT = "ZIPCODE = XYZ"
Ask user "Name of new file to write these names to?"
INPUT = "MAILFEB83"
Call up CUSTOMER to use for mailshot
Select records on ZIPCODE = XYZ
Write selected records to MAILFEB83
Prepare labels using MAILFEB83
```

Writing a Command File

A command file is created in very much the same way as a program is written. It is necessary to decide precisely what you want to do and to prepare small sections at a time, testing as you go and finally testing all the parts working together. However, there the similarity ends. Writing a command file for a database is much easier than writing a program, although it is hard to clarify exactly why this is so, especially when

talking to people who do not know what is involved in programming. When setting up instructions in a database, you
are thinking all the time about the information you want to
shunt around and what you want to do with it. You do not
have to get distracted by a concern for the type of file that is
going to be the most satisfactory, or any of those kinds of
advanced aspects of programming. For instance, if you want a
file to be indexed, you tell the base to index it. The decisions
about whether you should have a random access file or an
indexed sequential file have already been made for you by
the writers of the base. You made your decision when you
bought this particular base. Better still, you do not have to
struggle to understand and then write the best indexing algorithm. This decision too has been made for you. You simply
have to decide whether to index or not, and if so, which key
you would like to index on. In the light of your data, it should
be fairly easy to decide which key, and to read the page on
how to instruct the base to create an index. You also need to
be sure that it is being called into play on the occasions when
you are going to want it, and this should involve reading at
most one page of the manual.

Testing in Interactive Mode for a Command File

Naturally, the more complex the operations you wish to perform are, the harder they will be to organize even within a
command file. But another delightful aspect of at least some
bases is that you test each section out in interactive mode
before including it in the batch of instructions. This makes
the process more like using an interpreted language than a
compiled one (for those who know the difference to start
with).

For instance, you may wish, as part of a sequence of commands, to take a record selected on a given criterion from one
file, do some mathematical manipulation on a variable contained in the record, place it in another file, delete the original, and then find the next record that matches the selection
criteria and repeat the process. First of all, you would try

selecting a record from the original file on the chosen criterion. When that instruction was working correctly, you would add the mathematical manipulation of the variable. When the correct results were being produced, an instruction would be added to place the record in a second file. That file would be investigated to see whether the records were being added properly. Next the whole sequence would be tried, culminating in the deletion of the original record. Finally, when you were satisfied that the individual parts of the command work correctly, you would test the instruction by stepping through a sample file selecting record after record for processing in this way. At last the set of commands is ready to incorporate into a command file to be run as part of a batch of instructions. This would still need to be tested, but errors should now be easy to locate if they did occur.

The flexibility and scope given to a database by the facility for producing command files is something one could go on discussing and illustrating endlessly. My intention here is to help create some understanding of the concepts involved and a quick taste of the possibilities. Once you have grasped the notion of command files and begun to develop a feel for the use of this facility in databases, the limits of what can be done become far less rigid. The only caveat is that as the stringing of instructions together gets more elaborate, the speed of operation is reduced, and we are back to the problem of menu-driven programs—unacceptably slow speeds. However, a command file is not a straitjacket, and liberation and a return to direct interactive use of the base is always possible. Also, greater familiarity with the workings of the base may enable you to make improvements you were unable to appreciate as a beginner.

CHAPTER ELEVEN

Taking Data into Other Programs

From time to time I have suggested that there might be moments when it would be more sensible to use another program or package to extend the usefulness of the data that has been collected into the database. For this reason it is absolutely essential to choose a base that holds data in such a way that it is reasonably easy to get at it, see what it looks like, and transfer it to another program. The other side of this, of course, is putting into the base data that has been collected by other means, such as a data logging device of some kind—that is, a device for recording, or logging, data that is being read from some piece of equipment, like a gamma counter, or a device for reading pressures of any kind. I will discuss the more (though not very) difficult aspects of this later in the chapter; let's first examine the relatively straightforward operations.

Transferring Data to a Word Processor

The most frequent use for data from a database is as fodder for a word processor, either for a mailing list operation or for incorporation into an extended report, the bulk of which is text rather than filed or categorized items of information. As

time goes on, feedback from customers indicates to programmers and software developers the ways in which the provision
they have made falls short of what is needed in practice. The
first databases to be produced for use on microcomputers
were conceived in simple terms, and the notion of using a
word processor to shunt around the same information in order
to write reports, or to print names and addresses on standard
letters and envelopes, came only in response to complaints by
customers about the limitations. Traditionally the software
suppliers that were writing more and more skillful databases
were not the same as those that were concentrating on per-
fecting word processing packages. However, it became apparent that in order for a database to have any chance of
becoming a market leader, it must have a facility for preparing
a file of information in a form that could be picked up and
utilized by a word processor. In the different areas of microcomputing, separated mainly by the type of operating system
used by any given machine, one or another word processor
was tending to become a best seller; for these lucky packages
the database writers began to provide a defined utility that
would prepare the data on command without the user having
to learn the specifics of what was actually being done.

Delimiting Fields in a Record

If you are likely to want to get your data out of the base and
into a word processor not provided for, or into an unknown
package of any kind, then it is a good thing to check that there
is a more general utility for writing data out to some kind of
format that is flexible and acceptable outside the database.
This may be described in the manual as the ability to provide
an "external" format or a "delimited" file. The delimiters are
the characters that may be inserted into a file to mark the
beginning and end of each field and of each record. A field
may be delimited by something like a comma set between the
end of one and the beginning of the next. A record is nearly
always delimited by the carriage-return and a line-feed control character. Sometimes physical delimitation is unneces-

sary, since the program can calculate, on the basis of information it has been given, where the beginnings and ends of fields and records will fall.

Stage one of an operation to prepare a file for transfer is usually to remove the *header* from the database file, since it is peculiar to the base and would not be understood by another package. The header is the information that gives details of how the record is structured and held in the base. It may be a list at the start of the file, perhaps saying that there is a name field 30 characters long; a data field 8 characters long; a salary field 10 spaces long but filled with numeric, not character, data; and so on. This kind of list must be removed. If, as is sometimes the case, the header is held in a separate file, then life is simpler, since the data itself may need no alteration.

Although the new software package will need to understand the header information in order to make sense of the data, the header information will need to be translated into the codes that the new package expects and understands. Moreover, the few lines of header information at the top of a file are not in the same form as the rest of the file, which will be set out as records of data values, not field headings and sizes. Thus if the header information is the first to be encountered, the new program will be thrown by finding data that does not match the pattern it has been told to look for. A typical file with header information might be:

```
name:20:C,  address:30:C,  salary:10:N:2,  age:3:N:0,  active:1:L,
John Smith      22 Hill St Chicago              14500.00 34 T
Mary Brown      10 Brookside Rd Philadelphia    26000.00 43 F
etc
```

The first line gives the program information about the fields of the record that it is being asked to handle. This comprises, for each field: the name of the field; the number of spaces that it will occupy for each entry; the type of data—character, number, or logical; and the number of figures after the decimal point, if any. The next two lines contain actual data. The data has no delimiter, or marker, to tell the program the field is ended and another one begun. This is because, since it has been told that the first field is 20 spaces long, it does not need to be told when that field is ended. It can count for itself. Some programs operate this way, but some do not. For those that do not, a marker or delimiter is necessary to delineate the end of each field and the start of another. This may be necessary for either the file from which data is being sent or the one to which it is being passed, according to the requirements of each. If the delimiter were a comma, the same file might look as follows:

```
name:C, address:C, salary:N, age:N, active:L,
John Smith,22 Hill St Chicago,14500.00,34,T
Mary Brown,10 Brookside Rd Philadelphia,26000.00,43,F
etc
```

Some databases allow you to instruct them to prepare a data file without a header and with a delimiter of your choice, in order to make the data immediately acceptable and available to another program to read and interpret. Where the new form required is not a standard one, or where the database does not provide this facility, then it is necessay to write a little routine as a special program. Ways of doing this are discussed at the end of the chapter.

Transferring Data to Statistics Programs

First, however, let us look at some uses for data outside the base, other than those involving the ubiquitous word processor and mailing list. The joy of a modern database is that you can put the data into it in very much the form in which you ultimately wish to make use of it. Obviously, you may say, otherwise why would one use it? Traditionally data has been entered and stored in computers in a form very far from that in which it is eventually used. All kinds of coding methods, usually involving the numeric representation of data, have been devised in order to cram the data into a small space, or into a form that the more limited early programming languages could handle without difficulty. Improvements in the field have now made it possible to be more relaxed in our methods. For instance, it is useful when storing records about people for analysis at a later date to have an identifier that is more precise than a simple number. If records are to be used for two purposes, like patient records for a clinic as well as for research, then it will be convenient to list the names and addresses and other items of description in the form of words in order to be able to identify or write to patients individually. However, for research purposes it may be desirable to put some of the data through a statistical package in order to get quantitative indications or information about patterns of illness, etc. Statistics programs generally expect only numeric data. Thus it would be helpful if from a record that looked like this:

```
Number:          0568
Name:            James Brown
Address:         16 Wood Lane Sarasota
Age:             56
Sex:             1
Blood pressure:  1
Cholesterol:     1
Smoker:          0
Exercise rating: 5
Advice given:    Warning given 2/10/83. Diet 2 recommended.
Next appt:       03/24/83
```

it were possible to take off the numeric data only and have:

```
Number:          0568
Age              56
Sex:             1
Blood pressure:  1
Cholesterol:     1
Smoker:          0
Exercise rating: 5
```

This record is ready to go into a statistics package. In this form it will be a simple matter for the statistics package to count the number of men, recorded in the file currently under analysis, who have high blood pressure, who smoke, and who do not exercise. From this it may be possible to deduce a correlation between the general characteristics of lack of exercise and high blood pressure, or lack of exercise combined with smoking as an indicator of the likelihood of high blood pressure, etc. This is a simplistic example, of course. The data might still require some doctoring if the statistics package held data in a different form, but that is another problem, to be discussed later in this chapter.

Data for Graphics Output

Graphics design is another use for which the data from a general file might be wanted. Bar charts, histograms, and such can be produced quite simply from the numeric data from any file, thus representing graphically the information on patients, company productivity, business forecasts, etc. More elaborate data, such as readings from laboratory equipment or mathematical output of any level of sophistication, requires appropriate equipment for producing graphics and is altogether more complicated. However, useful graphics output must have useful data to work on, and there is every possibility that this data will be part of the same information that is being worked over in another way by a database. Thus we have the same requirement: to be able to extract the relevant items, or the whole file, from the base and translate the data, with the minimum amount of effort on the part of the user, into a form acceptable to the program that will use it and process it into pictures and visual aids. These can be incorporated into a written report, if there is a plotter and/or a printer that can produce graphics output. They can also be used on a screen that accurately reproduces the pictorial representation of data, and can be used to illustrate lectures, training sessions, and other such presentations.

More and more attention is being paid these days to computer graphics and the pictorial representation of information, since it is considered to have far more impact on the audience than mere words. For this reason it is essential that, given the work that goes into building up a database, data, once accumulated, should not be confined to any particular use but be available for all purposes.

Now let's turn to more complicated examples.

Forms in Which Data is Held

Although it is true to a considerable extent that it is unnecessary to be able to program in order to use applications programs or to know anything about how computers work, there are circumstances in which a little knowledge is an excellent thing. One of these circumstances is when you want to get data from one program into another one that holds the data in a different form, and for which there is no readymade transfer routine.

It is first of all necessary to grasp the fact that the way in which information is presented to us by the computer does not reveal the form in which it is actually held internally by the system. A line of text or figures is always translated from the coded form in which it is held internally, and it is never held in the form in which it appears to us. At rock-bottom base level it is held by electrical pulses, coded in written form as binary numbers, but there will be a higher level at which it is coded in a form that can be manipulated by the particular software that is being used. This varies from one program or operating system to another. Because these codes are second-level codes, they can be cracked in terms of the first-level code and recoded into the desired second-level code if necessary. Often, however, the rearrangement will be necessary only within the second-level code, in terms of which field delimiters are used, as described above.

ASCII (American Standard Code for Information Interchange)

Let us look first, before the confusion becomes total, at the different types of codes that a program is likely to be using. By far the majority of programs on microcomputers will use the ASCII code. This takes the original binary numbers and codes them into a set of 128 letters, numbers, punctuation marks, and other symbols referred to as characters. These characters are the ones we normally use when reading and writing. A number is therefore a character, though a character is not necessarily a number. A list of the codes for the 128 ASCII character set, giving decimal, hexadecimal, and ASCII representation, can be found in most manuals and textbooks, and is given at the end of this chapter. One tends to get familiar with the most frequently used ASCII codes, like the numbers from 0 to 9, which are 30 to 39 respectively. Capital letters also soon become familiar, though usually I have to look up the lowercase ones. A space is something that occurs all over the place and is represented in ASCII by the number 20.

I have just caught myself in the sort of assumption computer people are always making: what I have just written is true only if you are thinking or writing in hexadecimal numbers. The reason for wanting to do such a thing at all is that when you take a "dump" (see below) of a file, it will usually be a hexadecimal representation of whatever is in the file. All this may seem confusing, but once you have grasped the basic concept that *all* information is coded in one way or another, and often in a different way in different parts of the system, it begins to fall into place. I cannot go into a lengthy explanation of the hexadecimal number system here; I explained it in my first book, *Understanding Microcomputers* (NAL/Signet), and you will find an explanation, more or less comprehensible according to how lucky you are in your choice of author, in most books on microcomputing. Fortunately, it is not important whether you know how to translate from ASCII or decimal to hexadecimal numbers, because there are lists that give the codes in parallel, and you need to know about it only in order to read a dump of a file.

Dumping Files

The next concept to come to grips with is that of the file dump. *Dump* is another computer term that is illuminating once you understand it but obscure until that moment. When a file is displayed to the user through some piece of program software, it is safe to assume that it has been translated from its original form into a code that is comprehensible to someone who has no knowledge of binary, hexadecimal, or any other of the number systems other than decimal, and who expects to see letters as letters and punctuation marks as such, not as hieroglyphics. If the data was entered in the form of words, therefore, the codes that represent letters will be presented as letters and punctuation marks, etc. Some of the characters will not have a screen representation at all, since they will represent an action, such as a carriage return, that causes the next character to be placed at the beginning of a line, jumping to that position from the place where the last character was placed.

These control characters, as they are usually called, are not printing characters and can vary in interpretation from machine to machine. A standard tends to develop for the ones that are most frequently used, like carriage return.

Sometimes what we want is to see the exact contents of a file, not dressed up or interpreted for any kind of presentation. To get this it is necessary to perform a dump. Software is summoned to do even this for us—we can do virtually nothing without software—but it knows that we are interested now in the bare bones. It therefore lists the exact contents of the file, including the codes that normally cause an action to be performed. These codes are listed, and on this occasion they are not translated into action, so we can see precisely what is there and the order in which things have been entered. The dump is not presented in the original binary codes, since these are long-winded and hard to translate. It is nearly always represented in Hex, which is a halfway house between binary and decimal numbers, and, in this case, between binary and ASCII codes. The nicest software tools for doing this add a translation of each character into its ASCII equivalent. A typical dump of a file, using a program that gives us a legible translation as well, might be the listing below, which is of the lines of text that you are now reading.

41	20	20	74	79	70	69	63	61	6C	20	20	64	75	6D	← Hex representation
A			t	y	p	i	c	a	l			d	u	m	← Actual text
70	20	6F	66	20	61	20	66	69	6C	65	2C	20	20	75	
p		o	f		a		f	i	l	e	,			u	
73	69	6E	67	20	61	20	70	72	6F	67	72	61	6D	20	74
s	i	n	g		a		p	r	o	g	r	a	m		t
68	61	74	20	20	67	69	76	65	73	20	20	75	73	20	20
h	a	t			g	i	v	e	s			u	s		
61	20	0D	0A	6C	65	67	69	62	6C	65	20	74	72	61	6E
a		.	.	l	e	g	i	b	l	e		t	r	a	n
73	6C	61	74	69	6F	6E	20	61	73	20	77	65	6C	6C	2C
s	l	a	t	i	o	n		a	s		w	e	l	l	,
20	6D	69	67	68	74	20	62	65	20	74	68	65	20	6C	69
	m	i	g	h	t		b	e		t	h	e		l	i
73	74	69	6E	67	20	62	65	6C	6F	77	2C	20	77	68	69
s	t	i	n	g		b	e	l	o	w	,		w	h	i
63	68	20	69	73	20	0D	0A	6F	66	20	74	68	65	20	74
c	h		i	s		.	.	o	f		t	h	e		t
68	72	65	65	20	6C	69	6E	65	73	20	6F	66	20	74	65
h	r	e	e		l	i	n	e	s		o	f		t	e
78	74	20	74	68	61	74	20	79	6F	75	20	61	72	65	20
x	t		t	h	a	t		y	o	u		a	r	e	
6E	6F	77	20	72	65	61	64	69	6E	67	2E				
n	o	w		r	e	a	d	i	n	g	.				

Note that some numbers have letters under them. Some have a punctuation mark, and the number 20 represents a space. The two numbers that the ASCII code cannot translate into characters are 0D and 0A. These are control codes, or action codes, which tell the software to perform a carriage return (i.e., go back to the beginning of the line) and a line feed (i.e., hop down one line).

These are represented by dots in the translation table. A dot means an incomprehensible code. It need not be incomprehensible to you, however, since it is possible to discover what these codes mean in certain defined contexts. You will probably not come across any but 0D and 0A in a database file, since carriage return–line feed is the standard way of signaling an end of line or end of record.

The example above is a dump of a text file. A dump of a data file from a database will reveal which characters, if any, are being used as field delimiters and which characters are being used to mark the end of each record. The two files shown below use different methods of delimiting fields, but the same method—carriage return—is used to mark an end of record. Note that in the translation, the carriage return symbol, which can be identified by reference to the table of control codes for any given machine, is shown as a dot. This is because it is not a symbol that can be translated into a normal character in the ASCII table, but is a symbol for action. Where a code cannot be translated into an ordinary character, it is always represented by a dot.

First, here is the file as it would be presented as an ASCII listing:

```
Joan Brown,25 Hill St, Burlington,NJ,24,f,9000
Robert Jones,12 Green St,New York,NY,34,m,16000
Mary Pringle,7 Harrison Rd,Birmingham,AL,45,f,21000
```

Here is the dump:

```
4A  6F  61  6E  20  42  72  6F  77  6E  2C  20  32  35  20  48
J   o   a   n       B   r   o   w   n   ,       2   5       H
69  6C  6C  20  53  74  2E  2C  20  42  75  72  6C  69  6E  67
i   l   l       S   t   .   ,       B   u   r   l   i   n   g
74  6F  6E  2C  20  4E  4A  2C  20  32  34  2C  20  66  2C  20
t   o   n   ,       N   J   ,       2   4   ,       f   ,
39  30  30  30  0D  0A  52  6F  62  65  72  74  20  4A  6F  6E
9   0   0   0   cr  lf  R   o   b   e   r   t       J   o   n
65  73  2C  20  31  32  20  47  72  65  65  6E  20  53  74  2E
e   s   ,       1   2       G   r   e   e   n       S   t   .
2C  20  4E  65  77  20  59  6F  72  6B  2C  20  4E  59  2C  20
,       N   e   w       Y   o   r   k   ,       N   Y   ,
33  34  2C  20  6D  2C  20  31  36  30  30  30  0D  0A  4D  61
3   4   ,       m   ,       1   6   0   0   0   cr  lf  M   a
72  79  20  50  72  69  6E  67  6C  65  2C  20  37  20  48  61
r   y       P   r   i   n   g   l   e   ,       7       H   a
72  72  69  73  6F  6E  20  52  64  2E  2C  20  42  69  72  6D
r   r   i   s   o   n       R   d   .   ,       B   i   r   m
69  6E  67  68  61  6D  2C  20  41  4C  2C  20  34  35  2C  20
i   n   g   h   a   m   ,       A   L   ,       4   5   ,
66  2C  20  32  31  30  30  30  0D  0A
f   ,       2   1   0   0   0   cr  lf
```

Here is the dump, but with 00 0D 00 as the delimiter instead
of a comma:

```
4A 6F 61 6E 20 42 72 6F 77 6E 00 0D 00 20 32 35
J  o  a  n     B  r  o  w  n           2  5
20 48 69 6C 6C 20 53 74 2E 00 0D 00 20 42 75 72
   H  i  l  l     S  t           B  u  r
6C 69 6E 67 74 6F 6E 00 0D 00 20 4E 4A 00 0D 00
l  i  n  g  t  o  n           N  J
20 32 34 00 0D 00 20 66 00 0D 00 20 39 30 30 30
   2  4           f           9  0  0  0
0D 0A 52 6F 62 65 72 74 20 4A 6F 6E 65 73 00 0D
cr lf R  o  b  e  r  t     J  o  n  e  s
00 20 31 32 20 47 72 65 65 6E 20 53 74 02E 00 0D
   1  2     G  r  e  e  n     S  t
00 20 4E 65 77 20 59 6F 72 6B 00 0D 00 20 4E 59
   N  e  w     Y  o  r  k           N  Y
00 0D 00 20 33 34 00 0D 00 20 6D 00 0D 00 20 31
         3  4           m           1
36 30 30 30 0D 0A 4D 61 72 79 20 50 72 69 6E 67
6  0  0  0  cr lf M  a  r  y     P  r  i  n  g
6C 65 00 0D 00 20 37 20 48 61 72 72 69 73 6F 6E
l  e           7     H  a  r  r  i  s  o  n
20 52 64 2E 00 0D 00 20 42 69 72 6D 69 6E 67 68
   R  d           B  i  r  m  i  n  g  h
61 6D 00 0D 00 20 41 4C 00 0D 00 20 34 35 00 0D
a  m           A  L           4  5
00 20 66 00 0D 00 20 32 31 30 30 30 0D 0A
   f           2  1  0  0  0  cr lf
```

In the first example the field delimiter is a comma. In the
second it is a sequence of three characters—a null followed
by a carriage return and another null. This is not the usual
form of delimitation on a micro. The more normal form is a
comma or inverted commas, or, alternatively, no field delimiter, since the software concerned knows the size of each field
in advance and will handle the data correctly, fitting it appro-
priately into each one. It is likely, therefore, as was the case
with this data when it was taken from a large computer down
to a micro, that the receiving program or database will not
have a standard delimitation format to accept and translate the
data into something useable. It will be necessary to write a
little routine to read the data, character by character, and

change the unacceptable delimiting codes into acceptable ones. One way of doing this is to read the original file character by character and transfer the characters to another file. Read from file I and write to file II. Whenever a null is encountered, drop it and the following two characters and instead write a comma into the new file.

A short program in Pascal illustrates how this can be done (see Figure 11.1 on page 106). This particular program removes a single byte from the beginning of the file. It is quite common to have an odd number or two at the start of a data file—a sort of limited header information, giving the number of records in file and so forth.

The program then asks the user for the name of the file to read from and a name to write the new data to. It also asks for the number of variables, since there are no normal end-of-record markers. Because there are no proper carriage return-line feeds in the original file, and thus no end-of-record markers, it inserts these after counting fields to make sure that it has the correct number for each separate record. Every time it finds a null character it throws it away (by reading it, but not writing out to the new file); throws away the next two characters, carriage return, and null, which are also unwanted; and writes a comma to the new file in their stead. Thus we end up with data in a form intelligible to the software that we are about to use.

Data Held in Binary Format

Data likely to be used for mathematical procedures and calculations is often held in binary form, since it is possible to achieve a greater degree of accuracy with less processor or language power if numbers are in this form. Thus quite often data being extracted from a database representing a larger field of interest than that which is now being quantified must be translated from the ASCII form of the database to the binary format required by the statistics or math package. Usually the manual of the program that needs binary data will give you some advice on how to write a routine to do this.

```
program remove0d;
type    byte = 0..255;
var     num : byte;
        i, varnumber : integer;
        f,g : file of byte;
        fname, gname : packed array(1..14) of char;

PROCEDURE GETINFO;
begin
    write ('Name of file to read from? eg  B:EXTERN.DAT');
    read (fname); writeln;
    write ('Name of file to read to?       ');
    read (gname); writeln;
    write ('How many variables?'    );
    read (varnumber); writeln;
end;

begin
    getinfo;
    reset (f, fname);
    rewrite (g, gname);
    read (f, num);

    while not eof(f) do begin

        i: = 0;

        repeat



        read (f, num);
            if (num = $00) then begin
                read (f, num); read (f, num);



                write (g, $2C);



                i: = i + 1;
        end (if num)
        else write (g, num);


        until i = varnumber;




        write (g, $0d); write (g, $0a);
    end; {while}

end.
```

program remove0d; type byte = 0..255; var num : byte; i, varnumber : integer; f,g : file of byte; fname, gname : packed array(1..14) of char;	Set up variables and files
write ('Name of file to read from?...'); read (fname); writeln;	ask
write ('Name of file to read to?');	user
read (gname); writeln;	for file
write ('How many variables?');	names and
read (varnumber); writeln;	number of
end;	variables
getinfo;	set up
reset (f, fname);	named files
rewrite (g, gname);	
read (f, num);	discard byte
while not eof(f) do begin	process whole file
i: = 0;	set counter for vars
repeat	read chars until quota of vars full
read (f, num);	read char.
if (num = $00) then begin	if null,
read (f, num); read (f, num);	discard it & next two chars.
write (g, $2C);	replace with comma. Write to new file
i: = i + 1;	Add 1 to var number count
end (if num)	
else write (g, num);	Else write char to new file.
until i = varnumber;	when var num same as that given by user, put
write (g, $0d); write (g, $0a);	cr-lf to
end; {while}	mark end of record

Figure 11.1. An illustration in Pascal

Certainly the manual for one of the best-known statistics programs does. I do not give the example here, as it is in BASIC, a language notoriously hard to read, though not to write, and so it looks complicated and might be off-putting. However, it should be easy to get a programmer to do such a routine for you in a short time.

EBCDIC

This is a code used on large computers. If the data can be transferred via 8-inch floppy disks, the translation can also be done by a specially written piece of software called a reformatter. Some such programs have in the manual a conversion table for translating ASCII to EBCDIC and vice versa. In more complicated circumstances than this, it would be better to call in a professional programmer to do the work.

Nonstandard ASCII Codes

Some machines, like versions of the Commodore PET, have a peculiar variation of their own of the ASCII code. This is usually because they have a limited keyboard or instruction set, and in the case of the PET the translation is quite easy. The uppercase letters, numbers, and characters are the same, but the lowercase letters all require a constant of 60 Hex to be added to them. A translating routine simply needs to do this. Here we are concerned with the translation of the code for all characters represented in a nonstandard way, rather than the insertion or alteration of field delimiters.

Figure 11.2 is part of a program set up to read text files over from a word processor on the PET into a word processor on a different machine. It illustrates the principle of a simple translation from one code to another and an opportunity to escape from the rigid constraints of one piece of software or operating system into another.

The keynote when choosing a database is flexibility. Through experience with customers over several years I have come to value, more highly than almost any other characteristic, the possibility of transferring data relatively easily from

```
program petws;
type       byte = 0..255;
           filename = packed array (1..14) of char;
var        num : byte;
           e, f : file of byte;
           i : integer;
           ename, fname: filename;

PROCEDURE GETNAMES;
begin
    writeln;
    writeln ('What is the name of the WORDCRAFT text file? ');writeln;
    writeln ('Give it as <drive:filename>, e.g. B:TEST1.PWP ');writeln;
    read (ename); writeln;
    write ('What is the name of the WORDSTAR text file? ');
    read (fname);
    writeln;
end; {proc getname}

PROCEDURE READOVER;
var  i :  integer;                                          | read char
begin                                                       | if not ASCII
    read (e,num);                                           | replace with
    if ((num > = $01) and (num < = $1A)) then               | same + 60H
      begin                                                 |
        num : = num + $60;                                  | write to
        write (f, num);                                     | new file
      end
                                                            | else write
    else begin                                              | original char
        write (f, num);                                     | straight to
    end; {else}                                             | new file
end; {proc trans}

BEGIN                                                       | set up files
    reset (e, ename);                                       | with names
    rewrite (f, fname);                                     | discard
    for i: = 1 to 238 do                                    | header
      read (e, num);                                        | translate
    while not eof(e) do begin                               | the rest
      readover;                                             | from one
    end; {while}                                            | file to the
                                                            | other
                                                            | until file
    end; {while}                                            | is finished

end.
```

Figure 11.2. Translating a PET Wordcraft program to Wordstar

Character	Decimal Code	Hex Code	Character	Decimal Code	Hex Code
Space	32	20	@	64	40
!	33	21	A	65	41
"	34	22	B	66	42
#	35	23	C	67	43
$	36	24	D	68	44
%	37	25	E	69	45
&	38	26	F	70	46
'	39	27	G	71	47
(	40	28	H	72	48
)	41	29	I	73	49
*	42	2A	J	74	4A
+	43	2B	K	75	4B
'	44	2C	L	76	4C
-	45	2D	M	77	4D
.	46	2E	N	78	4E
/	47	2F	O	79	4F
0	48	30	P	80	50
1	49	31	Q	81	51
2	50	32	R	82	52
3	51	33	S	83	53
4	52	34	T	84	54
5	53	35	U	85	55
6	54	36	V	86	56
7	55	37	W	87	57
8	56	38	X	88	58
9	57	39	Y	89	59
:	58	3A	Z	90	5A
;	59	3B	[	91	5B
<	60	3C	\	92	5C
=	61	3D	]	93	5D
>	62	3E	↑ or ∧	94	5E
?	63	3F			

Figure 11.3. Decimal and hex codes for alphanumeric characters. The hex codes for lower-case letters of the alphabet require the addition of 20 to the hex codes for the capitals given above (e.g., a lower case O is 6F, and a lower case R is 72).

one base to another. If, through ignorance, lack of foresight, or changing circumstances, you choose a base that turns out to be inadequate for the present purpose, then you have lost only the price of the base—a few hundred dollars at most—if you make a change. If the data is held in an obscure way that makes it difficult or impossible to change, then at best you have lost the data completely if there is no paper record of it, and at worst you have to pay vast sums to have it keyed in all over again into another base.

CHAPTER TWELVE
The Future

I consider that databases in one form or another are, and will be even more in the future, the most important single form of computer application. The better ones are already being used almost as if they were high-level languages. High-level languages are the tools that many, if not most, programmers use when writing programs for applications software, that is software for a special application such as a betting system, an accounting package, a statistics program, a time-tabling system, or a graphics display. Systems software and the parts of applications that need to run especially fast are more often written in machine code. Machine code is much more difficult to write and is nonportable, that is, different for each individual machine. This makes it less desirable in many ways than a high-level language except for the jobs at which it excels. Such jobs are those for which speed is essential or a very compact code is a necessity, perhaps for small areas of memory in a piece of equipment using a processor but not a whole computer system, or, alternatively, for very small machines like the new hand-held portable computers. If a database is itself written in machine code or some intermediate language like Bell Labs' C, it can then be used in almost the same way as a language, allowing people who have not learned to program to simulate programming. Such people may be able to set up elaborate systems that make full use of the concepts of programming without having to have spent years being trained in their execution.

What other improvements and developments are likely to take place before databases become widely used? There are two main areas where development is necessary. The first is the interaction between the person and the database. This involves developments in the hardware—the equipment— and parallel developments in the software. People will never be entirely at ease with computers while everything has to be written down. Moreover, this cannot be avoided simply by clever use of the screen. There are ways now in which the user can point at objects displayed on the screen, to reduce some of the typing-in process. But with a database this can never be more than a very minimal aid. You can point only at things that you can see, and this limits the selection to items displayed on a menu, or something of a similar nature. Essentially, you are requesting the database to handle data by general blocking or grouped characteristics: "Find all items that correspond to this description and move them to such and such a location." You could point to such items only if the file were slowly scrolled before your eyes, which would take an eternity and make you dizzy—worse than microfiche, about which there are many complaints. The only method of communication that gets around this and does not involve things being written down is speech. Thus the machine's ability to respond to a spoken description is a prerequisite for truly mass use of databases and computers.

Speech recognition, or the ability of computers to understand and respond to the spoken word, is not in itself enough. Once people can talk to computers, they are not going to be disciplined enough to obey the current rather stilted rules of syntax and vocabulary that govern communication between person and machine. The software will have to have its own private database, a thesaurus of terms and expressions, so that it can translate for itself, sometimes resorting to questioning and answering the user in order to clarify a particular point and get to the vaguer and more ambiguous meanings of the spoken word. There is no reason why users should not be gently trained by the base in the use of special terms, so that, as they begin to remember the precise terminology, the base can respond more speedily to their requests and thus, without making the correct use of terms a prerequisite, present an incentive for improvement. The process can involve intelligence, sensitivity, and learning on both sides.*

Combining software currently applied to word processors with that used in databases would cause a different kind of breakthrough, involving a quantum leap in the software rather than an improvement in the area of interaction with human beings. If a database could handle long passages of text in "free format," like a word processor, and then quantify it— perhaps giving coded values to certain words or phrases, counting the occurrences, giving a heavier weighting to some than to others—it would become possible to evaluate text in the way that we now evaluate data. Some databases can handle text in free format—in blocks whose extent has not been predefined by fields of a given type or size. The kinds of processing that can be done at the moment on text, in either a database or a word processor, are all variations on the string searching, matching, and joining theme. Numbers of words can be counted, but values are not attached.

For many applications the actual evaluation of text would not be useful. There are instances, however, such as assessing 200 applications for a computer programming job advertised in the newspapers, when at least a preliminary assessment of a crudely quantified nature would be helpful. Without removing the element of human judgment from the assessment of candidates for jobs, a rough ordering of such things as education, professional experience, relevant languages, and so on would help to produce some kind of order out of chaos. It is quite possible, too, as skills in this use of word evaluation develop, that the language of a piece of text could be evalu-

---

* For an interesting, speculative discussion of this matter, see Neil Frude, *The Intimate Machine: Close Encounters with Computers and Robots* (New York: NAL Books, 1983).

ated as professionally as it is now by human assessors, with their widely varying tastes and opinions. Computers have been used to help detect whether or not a particular piece of text is the work of Shakespeare, by a comparison of literary style based on the frequency and use of certain words and phrases. Why, then, shouldn't evaluation, or rating and grading, of style take place? The fear is that the computer would apply lower standards than we would. But most people by "we" mean "I," and I would put the judgment of a well-trained machine as high as that of many people, including many of the guardians of our language such as teachers, some of whom are not as literate as we expect them to be. It is well known that standards of grammar and spelling have sharply declined among better-educated members of the population, even if general literacy is higher. Computers can be programmed to store information, but also to learn from experience. This characteristic could make it possible for a system to be flexible, and to adapt at the appropriate moment to new uses of vocabulary and idiomatic developments of language.

Any machine system must be open to intervention and correction by humans if it is to be acceptable. Here, as elsewhere, the important thing is to get computers to do the tasks that involve drudgery or are of a complexity beyond the reach of ordinary human calculation. The computer and the database together make an excellent assistant. With a little further training in how to speak politely and respond to ambiguous and badly-thought-out commands, we will have an assistant whose overtime will not have to be paid for at double rates, whose personal life will not be put under stress because of long working hours, whose vacations will be only short periods of recuperation, and who will be content to play with us when we are bored or short of work.

CHAPTER THIRTEEN
Conclusions

Most people, when they first use a microcomputer, begin with a relatively simple operation. The danger is that they will find a tool that, although it does the present job very nicely, cannot do much else. There is also the very serious risk of choosing out of ignorance something that does not do even the present job very well. It is therefore worth spending some time reading and thinking about what is involved, and what might later be useful, before making a purchase. One proud owner of a simple database told me the other day that most people did not want a relational database. I replied: "Most people do not know what a relational database is. They might very well want it if they realized what the possibilities were."

It is for this reason that I have tried to chart the potential uses, looking at more than the simple entry, storage, and retrieval of data, that can be obtained from a database running on a microcomputer. As I said at the start of the book, there are databases, running on larger machines, that manage to perform in a much more sophisticated way, but these are usually difficult to use as well as to understand. At that level there is an army of professional advisers to help the user, whereas with a micro you cannot get from the base any facility that you have not understood to exist, or that you have not understood how to invoke. The manual with any package will usually tell you what the software can do. (Even this is not always the case, but we probably have to assume it for the sake of peace of mind.) If you are familiar with the ideas and language, which I hope you are beginning to be after reading this book, then you will be able to put the base to good use. Without some preparation, either by having been in computing for some time or by reading what might in the jargon of the trade be called a "preprocessor," such as this book, you will find it difficult if not impossible to understand the further refinements of the software simply by studying the manual. This is a pity for all sorts of reasons, not least that you will not be getting value for money.

The influence of technical terms and jargon is so insidious that, in spite of the traumas I had in coming to terms with it myself, I now constantly find myself slipping into the use of it. I apologize retrospectively for all the lapses I have not spotted and remedied in this text. It is, however, necessary to concede that there are some words and technical terms with which it is necessary to become familiar. Language must develop to cope with unprecedented situations, to describe neatly and briefly items and events that are not part of our heritage but are part of our present and our future. We have to move with language as well as with the times, and we must learn the new words if we are to take in the new concepts and use the new technology. This can be a pleasure as well as a difficult task.

It is also a pleasure as well as a difficult task to learn about something as clever and useful as a good database. Future generations will be as familiar with the concepts as we are with the three—or, for many of us, the two—R's. Databases will come to be the foundation of nearly everything for which computers are used, and most people agree that computers will be at the center of nearly everything we do, sometime in the not-too-distant future. Without getting positively fervent about it, it is better to embrace the opportunities with enthusiasm than to concede with reluctance.

GLOSSARY

It is necessary to understand a certain number of terms that are frequently used in connection with databases. Even if these terms were to be avoided in this book, they would be encountered elsewhere. The following words and phrases are used throughout the book; they are listed and defined here for easy reference for moments of doubt and confusion.

batch mode A system for entering a lot of data or instructions rapidly, without any kind of dialogue between the user and the machine. No checking mechanisms are active, for instance, and the data is accepted uncritically. Later it can be cleaned and edited in some other way.

byte A space large enough to take one character or number. Its actual meaning is more complex but not relevant here.

constant A value that is not entered into a variable field but brought in from outside. For the duration of the present job, therefore, it does not vary but retains a constant value. An example is the rate of, say, 5 percent by which every value under the field heading SELLING PRICE might be multiplied, in order to produce a price that included a state's sales tax. The contents, or value, of the field vary with each record, but the multiplier stays constant at 5 percent.

cursor addressing or positioning Directing the cursor to a particular address on the screen. This may not be absolutely clear unless you understand what an address on the screen is: The

80 spaces of width and 24 lines of depth form a matrix that has 80 boxes running one way and 24 another. It is a matrix, or the area described by a Cartesian axis, whose individual locations can be addressed by an x,y coordinate. This is the equivalent of an address locatable by the correct row and column names. For instance, address 0,0 (just to be perverse) is the first box, identified by the first column and the first row on the screen. Figure G.1. shows other Cartesian coordinates on a matrix.

```
 |1 2 3 4 5 6 7 8 9 |
1 |1,1               1,9 |
2 |   2,2                |
3 |      3,3      3,7     |
4 |         4,4          |
5 |            5,5       |
6 |               6,6    |
7 |      7,3      7,7     |
8 |   8,2            8,8  |
9 |9,1               9,9 |
```

Figure G.1. A matrix with Cartesian coordinates

data management system A lofty phrase to encompass the shunting around of data in and between any of the containers described below, in order to get the maximum return from it.

default value A value the base will fill in for you if you do not give a specific answer to a question. For instance, a question such as "Do you want to have totals calculated on this field? (Y/N)" may have a default answer of NO. This means that if you merely press the carriage return key instead of finding the N key and pressing that, your answer will be assumed to be NO, in default of the specific answer YES. Default values for the number of lines wanted on a printed page, width of paper, and much more complicated things—such as whether your word processor will expect the printer to be set at 10 or 12 characters per inch—are usually filled in by the software as default, and you alter the defaults only where you definitely want some different value to be used.

field or variable The smallest whole division of data. Even this can be looked at in subsections occasionally, as with the function that asks whether a certain sequence of characters is to be found anywhere within a larger complete string. A field or variable must have a name in order to turn it from a generic concept into a specific identifiable container of information. The way in which such a name or heading can be defined will be stated by the rules of the database. It is common to have a maximum of ten letters or characters allowed. Thus the name of the first field of a list of names and addresses might be SURNAME. Often the field contents, or the value of the field, can be asked for in a more expanded way, such as "surname and initials (e.g., Brown JH)," but the actual field name for the base to manipulate would still have to be a restricted one.

file A collection of records, placed together into a single file, that can be manipulated and moved around as a single entity, identified by its file name, which must be unique on any given disk. For instance a file called PERSONALDAT might contain 1,000 records of individuals. The records might contain such fields as SURNAME, TITLE, SEX, AGE, LENSERVICE, SALARY, COMMISSION, PENSION, PREVEXPER, DEPARTMENT. The values in these fields could be looked at and processed individually, and the records as a whole could be processed, for instance to give a picture of the company personnel in statistical terms. The file could be linked to other files, or used by several different command files or other packages like word processors or accounts programs.

function An operator that is complex or made up of several operations. Multiplication is a simple operation. Finding a square root is a function, because it involves the use of more than one operation and more than one operator. Exponentiation is a function because, although it involves only multiplication, it is not simple multiplication of one number by another but the multiplication of a number by itself a given number of times. These details are contained in one symbol, which denotes the function.

indexing The method whereby a file of data is itself indexed for rapid retrieval of any record currently specified according to the rules of the index. This is different from a search or select feature, which is often confused in people's minds with indexing. It is also different from sorting data into alphabetical or any other intelligible order, since the ordering of an index is internal and not comprehensible to anyone outside the base.

interactive mode Involving interplay between person and machine. The program may ask for input, and the user will respond; the program may check the input and reply with messages, such as "Error in data, please check the range, which should be between 0 and 10," or "Next entry, or F to finish data entry." Or a menu of choices for the next action may be offered.

key A word used in various ways in computing. People talk about searching on keywords, using index keys, linking keys, and so on. In a database it is used to denote the field on which an operation such as sorting or indexing may be done. When a file is indexed, one particular field has to be chosen as the field that will be taken for every record and used for the index. The index is often kept physically separate from the whole file. For instance, a file of parts held in stock for a company may be indexed on an identifying field, which is then a unique number that also identifies the part to the user.

A file like that in Figure G.2 might be indexed in another file

Partno	descrip	qty	buyp	sell	sup	deliv
TS04461	chips	200	1.00	1.25	XYZ	3
DF54632	sockets	500	.50	.60	ZXY	2
BG87654	pcb	100	10.0	12.0	YXZ	4

Figure G.2. An example of a file

in another way (as in Figure G.3). The second file, in that case, would be used to find the relevant record extremely rapidly, and would contain, unseen by the user, a reference

```
IndexKey
BG87654   (ref to record)
DF54632   (ref to record)
TS04461   (ref to record)
```

Figure G.3. A reindexed file

to the whole record that would enable the base to get the full record instantly without lengthy search through the file.

macros Substitute identifiers, such as field names or file names. They are used to indicate the place where the full definition will be entered, probably interactively by the user. This device makes it possible to set up a general activity file that is put to a particular use on each separate occasion that it is called into action. The routine to sort a file might store a substitute for the file name and the sort key, and allow the user to define these differently and thus to sort different files on different keys whenever it is used.

menu A list of options, usually with a letter or number against each. If the appropriate key is pressed, the action for that option ensues.

operators

1. *arithmetic operators* The mechanism by which arithmetic operations can be carried out. There are four basic operators, from which, as with primary colors, other, more complex operations can be made up. The four make it possible to perform addition, subtraction, multiplication, and division. They are represented by the symbols $+$, $-$, $\times$, and $/$, respectively.

2. *relational operators* Operators that compare relative values rather than creating actual ones. The comparisons that can be made are whether a particular value is greater than another, greater than or equal to another, less than or equal to another, equal to another, or not equal to another value. These operators are particularly useful for the kinds of results that people require from a database, and their presence would in most cases be an important item to check for. In searches for certain items, the question will usually be whether there is a

record that has a value greater than a given constant (e.g., is salary greater than $20,000), but it might be whether there is a record where the value in one field is less than or greater than that in another (e.g., is selling price lower than buying price, thereby indicating that a tax deduction is in order).

3. *Boolean or logical operators* The operators that indicate whether a condition is so, whether it exists or not. The fact of a condition existing is indicated by a search criterion being met. The fact of two conditions existing is usually expressed in a way that uses the logical operators to check that condition *a* and condition *b* exist or do not exist, or that either one or the other exists. There are variations on this theme of *and, not,* and *or,* but these are the three basic operators. Some databases also allow Boolean symbols as types of data. Thus a field may have a value of true or false. No other value is allowed in a Boolean or logic field. Such fields can be used as flags to denote active or inactive cases, or the fact that certain important conditions are true or not true in the record under consideration.

4. *string operators* Used to manipulate letters of the alphabet and characters such as punctuation marks in a way similar to that in which arithmetic operators act on numbers. Strings can be added, or joined together, and this can be done in an exact form, leaving in what are referred to as "trailing blanks" or, in a compact way, removing all spaces. Searches can be made to discover whether a particular sequence of letters, or substring, occurs within a complete sequence, or string of characters. Strings, which can be number characters, can be turned into numbers and numbers into strings, for various reasons that may not be obvious here but can be very useful when manipulating data, e.g., when joining fields to make one from two, and so forth. String operators can tell us the position of certain items in a string of characters, and can pick out identified sets and operate on them. For instance, you might wish to take the fifth character of a sequence and the following three and compare them with some external value, in order to write out only part of a condensed piece of information. The

development of powerful string operators has recently revolutionized the use of databases on micros.

record The gathering together of fields as defined in a given file into a single entity; a collection of fields, connected by belonging to the same record and its identifier. Thus the several fields necessary to make up a personnel history are placed together in the structure of the file, and are manipulated or moved around as a single entity—the personnel record of X.

search or select A procedure whereby a record that matches characteristics described by the user can be searched for. These characteristics will not be simply the index field. They will be one or more fields, although, if more than one, they may include the index field. It should be possible to search on characteristics that do or do not exist, inclusively or exclusively.

sorting A procedure that sorts records into a stated order. This may be alphabetical, and the order of priority may be in ascending or descending order. Sorts may be on one field, or key, at a time or on several.

value or contents of a field or variable The entry made, for each record, under a given field heading. Although the field is the same for each record, the contents are different. Even where the contents appear to be the same, they are essentially a different item and therefore different. For instance, the entry of M for the word *male* under the heading SEX is the same value but a different item of data when it is entered against record number 0001 than when it is entered against record number 2003. One is record number:0001, field:SEX; the other is record number:2003, field:SEX. Although this seems obvious when thus illustrated, people get confused about the difference between the terms *variable* or *field* and their *contents*, which are properly the variable—or field— values.

variable type or data type The nature of the contents of a field. The entry may consist of characters, in which case it is a string of some kind; it may consist of numbers used as units of measurement rather than for some kind of ordering, as in street numbers; or it may be a logical type, giving a true or false result. Other data types can be made from these basic ones. For instance, number types can be split into whole numbers or numbers with decimal points. Dates can be allowed as a type if the base has an internal routine for calculating with dates.

INDEX

Reference Guides from PLUME

All about Computers from SIGNET and SIGNET DILITHIUM

(0451)

☐ **COMPUTERS FOR EVERYBODY by Jerry Willis and Merl Miller.** The comprehensive, up-to-date, easy-to-understand guide that answers the question: What can a personal computer do for you? Whatever your needs and interests, this book can help you find the personal computer that will fill the bill.   (128400—$3.50)*

☐ **BITS, BYTES AND BUZZWORDS: Understanding Small Business Computers by Mark Garetz.** If you run a small business, the time has come for you to find out what a computer is, what it does, and what it can do for you. With expert authority, and in easy-to-understand language, this essential handbook takes the mystery and perplexity out of computerese and tells you all you need to know.

(128419—$2.95)*

☐ **EASY-TO-UNDERSTAND GUIDE TO HOME COMPUTERS by the Editors of** *Consumer Guide.* This handbook cuts through the tech-talk to tell you clearly—in Plain English—exactly what computers are, how they work, and why they're so amazingly useful. Includes information needed to understand computing, to use computer equipment and programs and even do your own programming. A special buying section compares the most popular home computers on the market.

(120310—$3.95)*

☐ **KEN USTON'S GUIDE TO HOME COMPUTERS by Ken Uston.** In language you can understand—the most accessible and up-to-date guide you need to pick the personal computer that's best for you! Leading video game and home computer expert Ken Uston takes the mystery out of personal computers as he surveys the ever-growing, often confusing home computer market.   (125975—$3.50)

*Prices slightly higher in Canada.

**Buy them at your local
bookstore or use coupon
on next page for ordering.**

4c